MIRACLES &
MOMENTS
of GRACE

MIRACLES &
MOMENTS
of GRACE

INSPIRING STORIES FROM MOMS

BY NANCY B. KENNEDY

LEAFWOOD
PUBLISHERS

MIRACLES & MOMENTS OF GRACE
INSPIRING STORIES FROM MOMS

LEAFWOOD
P U B L I S H E R S

Copyright 2013 by Nancy B. Kennedy

ISBN 978-0-89112-404-7
LCCN 2012044938

Printed in the United States of America

Published in association with William K. Jensen Literary Agency, 119 Bampton Court, Eugene, Oregon 97404

LIBRARY OF CONGRESS CATALOGING-IN-PUBLICATION DATA
Miracles & moments of grace : inspiring stories from moms / Nancy B. Kennedy.
    pages cm
  Includes bibliographical references and index.
  ISBN 978-0-89112-404-7 (alk. paper)
  1. Motherhood--Religious aspects--Christianity--Anecdotes. I. Kennedy, Nancy B. II.
Title: Miracles and moments of grace.
  BV4529.18.M56 2013
  248.8′431--dc23
                                                                    2012044938

Cover design by ThinkPen Design, Inc.

Leafwood Publishers is an imprint of
Abilene Christian University Press
1626 Campus Court
Abilene, Texas 79601

1-877-816-4455
www.leafwoodpublishers.com

13 14 15 16 17 18 / 7 6 5 4 3 2 1

For all of us—

because we're the mom,

that's why!

Table of Contents

Introduction

After twenty-four hours of labor, Pam Guyer was exhausted. For two hours she'd been pushing, and yet her baby still had not been delivered. She'd had an epidural, but the pain had broken through anyway.

But at last, at 1 o'clock in the morning, one more push and Pam's labor was finally over. "It's a girl!" they told her.

"I cried when I heard my little girl's first cry," Pam recalls. "I thought, *Wow! Oh, my gosh. This is my baby!* She looked like she'd gone a few rounds with Rocky Balboa, but she was absolutely beautiful to me."

Both Pam and her husband were overwhelmed with exhaustion, so after Pam nursed her baby, the staff whisked her away to the nursery, giving the new parents a chance to rest.

A few hours later, Pam woke with an urgent desire to see her baby. "Let me just go see her!" she begged her husband. So, her husband wheeled her down to the nursery. The nurse held her up for the new parents to admire—Kaili, they had named her.

Back at her room, Pam drifted off to sleep again when she heard the sound of faint crying coming from down the hall. As she struggled to shake off sleep, the crying came closer and closer. Suddenly, Pam woke up with a startling knowledge.

"That's Kaili! That's Kaili crying!" she cried out to her husband. Pam had only heard her baby cry once, and yet she knew the sound of it instantly.

"My heart responded before I was even awake," Pam says. "The minute I heard that cry, I needed to hold my baby. The need was so intense, it was almost a pain."

Sure enough, a nurse came into the room, carrying her wailing baby.

"She's not a happy camper, Mom," the nurse said, apologetically. "We tried everything. We passed her around, but nothing we've done has soothed her."

Pam took her baby from the nurse's arms and began rocking her, talking softly to her and kissing her tiny features. Immediately, Kaili became calm and relaxed into Pam's arms.

That moment is etched in Pam's mind forever. It was a defining moment for her. *I get it now!* she thought. *We belong together. She knows me. I know her.*

Pam is the mother of three children now.[1] She and her family live north of Boston, and yet her experience could have happened anywhere in the world. Talk with almost any mother, and you'll hear a similar story of the instinctual, almost primal, bond of motherhood.

For this book, that's exactly what I have done—talked with mothers about motherhood. Within these pages, you'll find fifty stories from women who share with us the most memorable moments of their lives as mothers.

"When you have a child, you're not just giving birth to a baby," Pam says. "You're giving birth to a whole new role—a role that is unlike any other."

This new role, this identity, is often one for which we are unprepared. While an instinctual one for some, the motherhood role makes other women feel insecure.

"I didn't get a copy of the manual. I didn't know how to be a good wife and mother," says Jennifer Scott, a mother in Rome, Georgia. "I longed for a husband and children, and to create a God-fearing home, but I was a rookie. I just didn't know how to do it."

When you read Jennifer's story, you'll find that she is doing just fine, even without a manual. And even women who feel totally unsuited to motherhood—not just unprepared—seem to find a mother's heart beating within.

The author Anne Lamott worried that she might be "too self-centered, cynical, eccentric, and edgy" to raise a child.[2] Yet at her first ultrasound, after her doctor begins the scan of her baby, her heart suddenly overrules her head.

"He pointed out the vertebrae, a sweet curved strand of pearls, and then the heart, beating as visibly as a pulsar," Anne writes, "and that was when I started to cry."

A moment like Anne's sneaks up on many moms, often in the midst of an ordinary day. Perhaps when you're cooped up with your children on a rainy day or when you're picking up a child from school. One woman in this book shares a luminous moment with her son in the dairy aisle of a supermarket. Our children unknowingly provide us with moments of laughter and enlightenment—very often at the same time.

These moments resonate with us moms because we've all been there. As Pam Guyer says: *We get this!* We know what a mom's life is like—hectic, chaotic, challenging, and sometimes, yes, mind numbing.

Yet somehow, in the end, all the inconveniences, the anxieties, the struggles, the uncertainties fade, until what we have left in our memories are those fleeting moments that leave us in awe of our children and of the job of motherhood.

I think what makes this book, the third in the Miracles & Moments of Grace series, different from the others before it is exactly that element of common experience. In my two previous books, I shared inspiring stories from military chaplains and from doctors.[3] Their stories fascinated me because I had never experienced anything remotely like what these chaplains and doctors had gone through. I had never been in an operating room, had not been in a combat situation. Their stories provided a look into worlds I had never seen.

In this book, I found the reverse to be true. I found my mothers' stories fascinating precisely *because* I've experienced what these women have experienced. I've been through childbirth; I've lost sight of my toddler in a store; I've been reduced to a mound of mush by a loving look from my child.

In fact, while I was asking everyone else about their memorable moments, I couldn't help but turn the question in on myself: What has been *my* most memorable moment as a mother? And almost immediately, I had my answer. I hadn't thought about this moment for years, but it had come to mind once before when I was on vacation.

Every year in May, I get together with several girlfriends from college. We spread out in an airy four-bedroom house in Avalon, New Jersey, a shore town that I absolutely adore. Just hearing its name lowers my blood pressure by a few points! We spend our days in a leisurely haze, walking, biking, talking, cooking.

One year, as we were walking along the beach, we talked about *After Life*, a movie whose premise is that a person can enter heaven only after deciding on one perfect moment on earth to take with them into eternity.[4]

When one of my friends asked me what moment I would choose, I was surprised by the one that sprang instantly to life. At the time I didn't know it was even in my memory.

One year, when our son was 4 years old, we went on vacation to London. My husband and I had been to the city many times—he studied there one year—and we wanted to enjoy some time in this wonderful city with our son. It was definitely a different experience to spend our days going to places like the Diana, Princess of Wales Memorial Playground instead of Kew Gardens!

One day, we took the train from Paddington Station to Windsor. Our destination? Not Windsor Castle, unfortunately, but the shuttle bus to Legoland. *Where else?*

Now, I am a person who loathes amusement parks. Frankly, it's my life's loftiest goal to never step foot in Disneyland. (My poor deprived son will just have to wait for a youth group or marching band trip!) But Evan begged us and there was no schlepping him to another cathedral or museum until we gave in to his Lego obsession.

It was a warm summer day in London—not hot, by any means!— but it was the first sunny day the country had enjoyed after weeks of its infamous rain and damp weather. Absolutely everyone was heading for Legoland! The shuttle bus was packed. The lines at the entrance gate snaked along for seemingly a mile. It had taken us three hours just to get from our flat in Maida Vale to the entrance gate of the park. I was ready to turn around and leave right then.

Once inside, we hiked around from ride to ride only to face similarly daunting lines at each one. An hour at least. With a 4-year-old in tow, that just wasn't an appealing idea. I dislike standing around with an antsy child waiting for something to happen—the Changing of the Guard was not on our itinerary this trip.

But in our quandary, we happened on one ride whose line seemed to be moving rather quickly, and so we took our place in the queue.

The ride was actually a driving course. A maze of roads was laid out in a town-like setting and, after a brief driving lesson, the riders were let loose in kid-sized electric cars, driving in the left lane (it was Britain, after all!), negotiating roundabouts, pulling up at stop lights, motoring down straightaways. The line moved relatively fast because a dozen or so drivers took to the road at a time in their blocky, primary-colored Lego cars.

Evan's eyes lit up when he saw kids his age zipping around on the Lego roads. From the time he stood up and began to walk, Evan has always been all about motion. He desperately wanted to drive something . . . *anything*. Go karts, bumper cars, golf carts. You name it, he wanted to drive it. He had a bright red, battery-powered jeep that we let him steer up and down the sidewalks in town. But this . . . this was a whole new world for him!

Evan could barely wait for his turn. Sure enough, within fifteen minutes, he was seated crisscross-applesauce, listening raptly to the driving instructor. After the lesson, he was the first kid to jump into his car, a bright blue one, his favorite color.

My husband and I leaned on the gate, watching our mini Earnhardt wheel around the course. He was so intent he never even looked our way. He actually turned out to be a pretty good driver, cautious in the turns and roundabouts, and even ending up in the correct lane—no small feat when you're driving on the left side of the road. He was confident enough to pass a fellow driver whose car had stalled, and he even remembered to signal his turns. (Though Evan says he does remember running a red light!)

The kids got a good long ride, maybe ten minutes or so, before they were summoned to pull their cars into the gate. Evan hopped out of his car and headed for the exit. He spilled out onto the sidewalk and spied me a few yards away. Grinning crazily, he ran straight for me, his adorable little baseball sneakers barely touching the ground with each step. At the last second, I realized he was going to jump, and I opened my arms. He leapt into my embrace and hugged me tight, his small arms encircling my neck, his chubby legs wrapped around my waist.

This was it. My perfect moment. It was an electrifying moment of pure joy. Until that moment, I honestly don't think that I had ever felt like a mother. I had always felt like a person who just happened to be carting around a child. My husband and I used to joke about it. "When are this kid's parents going to come and get him, anyway? We've had him for a long time now," we'd say. (Not within Evan's hearing, of course!)

If I'm honest, I have to admit that I had ambiguous feelings about motherhood all along. I came to it late—I had my son at age 41. That's a lot of life to live without being a mom. Maybe it was just exhaustion, but I just couldn't seem to take pleasure in all the small moments that other women swooned over. It made me question whether I really had it in me to be a mother.

But in that moment, I suddenly and unexpectedly experienced that miraculous connection, that primal, not-to-be-denied clutch of love that claims a child as your own. I blinked back my tears, tried to hide them, knowing that Evan wouldn't see them for what they were— tears of my heart-deep happiness.

In that most unlikely of places, I finally knew without a doubt that I was a mom. And not just any mom, I was *Evan's* mom. It was a moment of pure delight for me. No other emotions were competing for my attention. My inner conflicts were stilled. The frustrations of the day fled. It was just Evan and me, sharing this magical moment of childish excitement.

Although it felt like time was standing still, I'm sure it was just a matter of seconds before I put Evan down. I'm not a weight-lifter by any means! But that moment lived on in my subconscious, resurfacing easily years later as I walked along the shoreline talking with friends about our perfect moments on earth.

If I hadn't been a mother, I would have looked for my perfect moment elsewhere—there has been no lack of them in my life. But most moments of our lives, no matter how happy, seem to be clouded with emotions that make pure joy nearly impossible. The anxiety that attends a wedding day. The frustration that accompanies travel. The sadness of our fleeting moments, no matter how happy they make us in that instant.

It's ironic that my perfect moment happened in a place that I had convinced myself would make me totally miserable. In fact, in *After Life*, the movie I mentioned earlier, a young girl who is deciding on her perfect moment is dissuaded by a guide from choosing a moment at Disneyland. Too many people choose those kinds of moments, the guide gently chides. I don't care what they say! Legoland will forever remain a precious place for me.

Yet, despite transcendent moments like mine, we all know that motherhood is not all tea parties and teddy bear picnics. Motherhood is one tough assignment. Many of the moms you will meet in this book have struggled. They've struggled with devastating loss, post-partum depression, physical disabilities, and life-threatening health conditions.

For these women, memorable moments have been dramatic and often heartbreaking. One woman tells of experiencing a horrific car accident while three months pregnant. Another woman goes into near-fatal cardiac arrest in childbirth. These moms have faced the toughest moments of motherhood and come through all the stronger for it.

Not only can motherhood be physically challenging, but it presents unique emotional challenges as well. From the moment a child is born, a woman navigates the world with a heightened sense of exposure. She is no longer wholly contained within herself—her boundaries of space and time are dissolved.

"Making the decision to have a child is momentous. It is to decide forever to have your heart go walking around outside your body," says Elizabeth Stone, an author, professor, and mother of two.[5]

Dr. Stone's observation is no mere academic musing. The week before she voiced this observation, she had rushed her young son to the emergency room twice in one night. A bacterial infection had caused the soft tissues of his throat to swell, closing off his epiglottis and threatening to suffocate him.

Her son pulled through, yet the experience left Dr. Stone with a new sense of a mother's calling. It is what she calls her "Pietà" understanding of motherhood.

"Motherhood encompasses both joy and an overwhelming sense of vulnerability," she said to me.

"Mary was privileged to be the mother of Jesus, but she also suffered," she continued. "She was at the foot of the cross at Christ's death. Suffering is an unavoidable part of motherhood."

In fact, from the very beginning of Mary's life as a mother, she experienced this inner conflict of joy and suffering. When she and her husband, Joseph, presented the baby Jesus at the temple in Jerusalem, the prophet Simeon told the new mother, "A sword will pierce your own soul."[6]

Yet Mary was not left alone in her suffering. Sharon Betters, a mother who tells a heartbreaking story of loss in this book, pointed out to me that after Simeon foretells Christ's death, the prophetess Anna, an elderly widow, approaches Mary to comfort her and give thanks to God for her son's life of redeeming power.

Until Dr. Stone mentioned Mary's presence at the foot of the cross, it never really struck me that her agony was no less diminished by the fact that Jesus was an adult in his 30s at the time of his death. A mother's connection with her children doesn't fade with time. In fact, as mothers spoke with me, it was sometimes hard for me to tell how old a woman's children were by the way she talked about them.

"When my son was out of my sight, I worried about him," admits Penny Reeder. "The world is a dangerous place and I couldn't help but think, *Is my baby all right?*" At the time, Penny's son was in his 20s and living on his own. In her story, she voices her concern for her "boomerang child," and how she sought solace in prayer.

As Mary did in her moment with Anna, many women have been privileged to experience times of spiritual clarity in motherhood. Women view these moments of grace as gifts from God, but at the same time, they may arise out of this dichotomy of joy and fear, and often out of deep suffering. One woman shares what she calls her "miracle moment"—the time a friend graced her with an astonishing kindness on the anniversary of her son's death. Another mom tells of a moment she woke in the middle of the night with an urgent need to pray for her son, and what she learned later about that moment.

I want you to know that all of the stories you will read in this book are absolutely true. In some cases, mothers chose not to reveal the names of their children in order to protect their privacy. A few women chose not to give their exact location and one mother used a pen name. But beyond that, nothing about the stories is fictional.

The stories in these pages have differing origins. In many cases, I interviewed the moms and told their stories in their own words. Some women wrote their own stories expressly for this book, and some had previously written about their moments in books, articles, or blogs, which I adapted here. A few stories were published previously in anthologies like Chicken Soup for the Soul. If a story has appeared elsewhere, I have noted its origins in the writer's biography that follows it.

After talking with mothers for the past year, I would say without a doubt that you don't need to convince any of the mothers within these pages that Ms. Stone's "Pietà" observation of motherhood is true. We all live our terrifying double lives of joy and fear. You certainly don't have to convince me of it.

The other day, my son told me that for his fourteenth birthday he wants to take a three-lap ride in a stockcar around Pocono Raceway at 180 miles per hour. Yes, really, someone in the NASCAR hierarchy— who I have no doubt is *not* a mother—thinks that this is a perfectly fine thing for my fragile child to do.

I can assure you that upon hearing these words, the moment of perfect joy that I experienced on the sidewalk at the Legoland driving school those many years ago morphed into a moment of perfect terror. Sometimes I wish this kid of mine would just stop walking around outside my body! Or, driving around, more accurately.

Nancy B. Kennedy
Spring 2013

**A grand adventure
is about to begin.**

—Winnie the Pooh

1

GOD BELIEVES IN MOTHERS

ANDÉ PEÑA

OAKLAND, CALIFORNIA

A mother is she who can take the place of all others
but whose place no one else can take.

CARDINAL MERMILLOD

My husband and I were on our way out the door for one of our "Funday Mondays," the night of the week when we ignored the dishes, the laundry, and the bills, and our only priority was to have fun together.

That night, it was as if a movie crew had set the stage. It was a warm summer evening, the crickets were chirping, the sun settling gently into the landscape. We were on our way to a romantic movie, and my protruding belly announced proudly that we were expecting our first child. Because I was seven months pregnant, I made an extra trip to the bathroom before we left. That's when someone on the set should have yelled, "CUT!"

In the bathroom, my water broke.

Suddenly, our outing was to an entirely different destination. When we arrived at the hospital, a nurse led us to a room and handed me the standard to-do list. She seemed unconcerned that I had gone into labor two months early. But soon a team of nurses hooked up monitors to track my contractions.

The doctors said they wanted to give me steroid shots to boost my son's lung function. I balked at this. Like many expectant mothers, I had been on a serious health kick throughout my pregnancy, eating organically, doing prenatal yoga, playing classical music on a headset cradled around my belly. I was traumatized by the idea of injecting steroids. We called a doctor friend to ask his opinion.

"The alternative is worse," he gently affirmed.

We signed the paperwork and I submitted to the first of many shots. I was also given medicine to stop the contractions and placed on complete bed rest.

For a week, everyone did what they could to keep my labor from progressing. But I developed toxicity to the medicines used to stop my contractions, and by the end of the week there was nothing else the doctors could do. I was taken off all medication, and soon our son Jonas entered the world at just 30 weeks gestation.

When the nurse placed him on my chest, I experienced a moment of pure bliss. He was perfect! He was just 4 pounds, 11 ounces, but he was beautiful, wiggling, and cooing softly. *Maybe he's going to be okay after all,* I thought.

Then my perfect, beautiful baby boy started to foam at the mouth.

The staff took Jonas from my arms and swept him out of the room, followed closely by my husband, my mother, and my best friend. I was left alone in the room with my doctor.

Everything grew quiet. My doctor spoke softly to me as she stitched me back up, but I didn't speak at all. I was numb, both physically and emotionally. And, I was angry. Angry because I'd done everything I was supposed to do, and it didn't matter. Angry because my hopes were dashed. Angry because my baby had to suffer.

More than that, I was scared for my baby.

It was more than an hour before I was able to make my way to the neonatal intensive care unit. The nurses tried to prepare me for what I would see, but I blocked them out. *If I don't acknowledge it, it won't be true*, I told myself. *He'll look like those chubby, healthy babies in the movies.*

The nurse wheeled me in and I stood up, balancing weakly against my wheelchair. What I saw broke my heart.

My son lay helpless in an isolette under a heat lamp, hooked up to monitors. An oxygen mask covered his tiny face and tubes led from his body to a bank of machines that beeped incessantly. He was curled up on his back, not crying or making any sound at all. It worried me how quiet he was. *Is he able to survive, or are these machines keeping him alive?*

Even worse was knowing I couldn't do anything for him. Every instinct in my body told me to pick him up and cradle him in my arms. I wanted to hold him, breathe with him, be one with him again—heal him!—but there was nothing I could do.

I felt defeated, hurt, angry, and useless. And, I felt a crushing sense of guilt. *Did I do something wrong?* I hadn't been a mother for more than a few hours, and already I felt like a failure.

My husband tried to allay my fears. "Jonas is doing great," Joel assured me. Still, my tears flowed. Joel squeezed my hand.

"Jonas is a fighter, Andé, and he can't be the only one fighting right now," he said. "He needs us to be strong, too."

Hard as it was, I decided right then to join the fight. I began to pray for strength. No matter what the outcome, no matter how difficult the journey, I determined that I would not surrender another moment of precious time with my son to fear and worry.

I would call on that prayer two days later when I was discharged from the hospital and had to leave my son there. When they told me my baby was not coming with me, I was shocked. *What kind of mother would leave her child?* I dreamed up totally nonsensical plans to stay with him, like *I'll hide out in the bathroom*. But in the end, my husband and I drove home alone, late at night. I cried the whole way home.

Jonas was in the hospital for a month. Our days were filled with endless medical tests. On good days, we celebrated his small accomplishments. On bad days, we suffered through complications and setbacks.

Finally, the day came to take Jonas home. I was excited and full of energy, not quite able to believe the day had come. At home, I isolated him and myself. *You want to see the baby?* You'll have to scrub up first. No entry to anyone who's been sick in the last decade or so!

Today, seven years later, Jonas is a healthy little boy. Although he has had more doctor appointments and more trips to the emergency room than the average child, he has met all of his developmental milestones. We are blessed beyond measure to be his parents.

When I question why my son's birth and early life had to be so difficult, I can only come to one conclusion: God must have had a lot of faith in my husband and me. I believe that God doesn't give us more than we can bear. He must have thought I was exactly the mother

Jonas needed. I want struggling mothers everywhere to know that God believes in us. God believes in mothers.

Andé Peña shares life with her husband, Joel, and their two children, Jonas and Kamila, alongside a vibrant circle of family and friends. Born and raised in Northern California, she graduated from California State University, East Bay, with a degree in sociology. She is currently the general manager for her family's textile recycling business. Through her volunteer work, she advocates for children, focusing on justice, education, and family counseling. Her blog, Living Out Loud, can be found at www.andepena.com.

2

MEETING BELLA

ANNE KIMBALL

OXFORD, PENNSYLVANIA

"Mom?"

"Hmmm?"

"Tell me a story."

"What kind of a story?"

"A story about the day we met."

"You're not too tired?"

"No, I'm not too tired! Please tell me."

"Well, OK. If you're sure . . ."

Many years ago, you lived on the other side of the world in the country of Kazakhstan, in a big building called the Detsky Dom, the Children's Home. You lived there with many other children and with the caregivers that the children called Mamas.

Now, these children were all different ages, all different colors and shapes and sizes. But you all had one thing in common. None of you had a family of your own. Sure, you had plenty of food, and things to do, and lots of children to play with. You had warm clothes and tights and shoes to wear, even if sometimes the shoes were too small or had holes where your toes would peek out.

But every once in a while you would have to say goodbye to one of your friends, because a new Mama and Papa wanted them to be part of their family. You didn't know why the children were chosen by these Mamas and Papas. Did they choose Anastasia because she had beautiful long blonde hair and eyes as blue as ice? Did they want Peter because he was so good at marbles and had that smile that made you smile right back?

You wondered if maybe one day a Mama and Papa would come for you. But you worried that no one would. You didn't think your teeth were pretty and you didn't like your short brown hair and the other kids said you talked funny and they teased you sometimes.

So you watched the Mamas and Papas come and go, and you said goodbye to many of your friends over the years. Still, you waited and you wondered and you dreamed.

Then one day, one of the caregiver Mamas had some news for you. She said that a Mama was coming to the Detsky Dom to see you. She was coming because she wanted you to be her daughter. This Mama would be coming in the morning.

At first you didn't believe her. It seemed too good to be true! You thought surely she must have meant Katarina with the beautiful braids. But the caregiver Mama assured you that she meant you. Bella.

That night was the longest night of your life. You had so many questions, questions that you didn't know the answers to, and sleep was impossible. What would your Mama look like? What would she smell like? Would she be soft? How would her hair feel in your fingers? Maybe she was a princess and wore a sparkly crown. Maybe she was . . .

At long last, you fell asleep.

When morning came, you jumped out of bed while all the other children were still deep in sleep. You sneaked quietly over to the window and sat there, looking out, staring at the place where cars come in off the street so you would be sure to see your new Mama the minute she arrived.

Sometime that morning, one of the caregiver Mamas came in to get you dressed. She slipped a dress over your head—a fancy red dress, all ribbons and lace. She brushed and smoothed your hair and made it pretty as could be with a white bow that was as big as your head. She gave you clean white socks and pretty buckle shoes that were—ouch!—too tight.

As soon as she was done, you went right back to your spot at the window. You waited and watched there all morning, for hours and hours.

Finally, the caregiver Mama came in and told you that it was time. She took you by the hand and led you out of the room, along the hall, down the stairs, and through many more hallways until you came to the director's office. Without hesitating, she sent you right in, giving you a little nudge to get you going. You took a few small steps inside the door and then you stopped, frozen with uncertainty.

There, across the room, sitting in a chair by the director's desk, was your new Mama.

She was wearing a long, flowy skirt and she had long, flowy hair. She smiled at you, and her eyes got all watery. You smiled back, but you didn't move from your spot by the door.

The director told you to come over and say hello to your Mama, and then she said to the Mama that you were shy. Then another lady, someone you didn't know, said something to the Mama in funny words that you didn't understand.

When still you didn't move, the grown-ups all went back to talking. But the Mama kept looking back at you and smiling. After a few minutes, you took a few steps toward the Mama. She was listening to the other grown-ups, but now and then she would look over her shoulder at you and smile some more.

You liked that smile, so you took a few more steps. You were almost close enough to reach out and touch her. A little closer and you were standing right beside her. She looked at you, and she put her arm around your shoulder, and she gave you a little pat.

You didn't realize that you had been holding your breath, but now you let it out like a sudden gust of wind. Moving ever so slowly, you backed yourself up until you were sitting right in the Mama's lap. She put both arms around you and started stroking your hair, and she rocked gently back and forth. You reached out to feel her hair, and it was just as you imagined—soft as silk.

You lay your head down on her shoulder and ran your little fingers through her hair, top to bottom, over and over. When you looked back at the Mama's face, you saw that more than just her eyes were watery. Her whole face was sloppy wet as tears washed down over her cheeks.

But somehow the tears didn't scare you. Although it seemed unreal, the Mama was crying because she was happy that she was your Mama. Not a caregiver Mama, not a princess Mama, but the best kind of Mama—a *real* Mama. Someone out there in the world beyond the Detsky Dom wanted you over all the other children in the whole wide world. She was yours and you were hers.

The thought that this Mama wanted you and loved you—you! Bella!—began to soak into your skin and into your bones and into your soul. It was like a warm spring rain seeping into the hard, icy ground of winter.

And as the Mama rocked you back and forth, stroking your hair with her warm hands and humming a quiet little song in your ear, you knew quite suddenly that you had found her. You had found your Mama.

And that Mama was Home.

Anne Kimball and her husband, Fred, a trauma surgeon, have six children, three of them adopted from Kazakhstan. They live on a farm in Oxford, Pennsylvania, in the middle of Amish country. Anne is writing a book about two disorders that can afflict adopted children—post-traumatic stress disorder and reactive attachment disorder. She blogs about her life and interests at Life on the Funny Farm (www.annesfunnyfarm.blogspot. com).

3

DRIVEN TO PRAY

DEB LING
SACRAMENTO, CALIFORNIA

I remember my mother's prayers
and they have always followed me.
They have clung to me all my life.

ABRAHAM LINCOLN

I was a single mom, and because of that I had a very close relationship
with my son. In fact, I could pretty much tell when he was going to be
sick hours before the first fever ever struck!

Well, my son grew up, as sons do. Dennis married and started a
family. He worked in Florida as a driver for a moving company. On
the job, he traveled long distances and often drove large box trucks
across the state.

One time, he dropped off his daughter to stay with me while he did
an overnight drive. After I'd gotten my granddaughter to bed for the
night, I drifted off to sleep myself. I'm a solid sleeper and rarely wake
up in the night.

On this night, however, I woke up at 2:30 A.M. with a start. A pressing thought bore down on me: *I have to pray for my son.* I have a strong relationship with the Lord, but this kind of thing had never happened to me before. So I knew I needed to act.

When Dennis was young and lived at home, I always prayed for a hedge of protection to surround us whenever we got in the car. Many times, we encountered situations in which we knew the Lord had kept us safe from danger.

Now, in the middle of the night, certain of my son's need for protection, I claimed the same promise from the Psalms that I had always stood on. "A thousand may fall at your side, ten thousand at your right hand, but it will not come near you" (Ps. 91:7).

After I had prayed, I felt a great sense of release. Knowing that everything was well, and free from any load of worry, I went back to sleep.

The next morning, Dennis came by to pick up his daughter.

"How was your trip?" I asked him.

He told me that he had had a close call during the night. Driving a large moving van, he hit a big rock in the road, causing him to swerve sharply and almost roll the truck. At the last minute, he was able to right the truck and keep it from going off the road. A chill came over me.

"Dennis . . . what time of night was this?" I asked.

"It was 2:30 in the morning, Mom. Why?"

Deb Ling, who lives in Sacramento, California, calls herself "The Praying Mom." She has written and published several e-books, including The Walking Wounded, *a book for women who have been abused, and* The

Wounded Soldier, *a book for men who have been traumatized. Both books are accompanied by workbooks. You can read more about Deb and see her e-books at her website Christians Be Healed (http://tinyurl.com/ Healing4U).*

4

In Memory of the Fish

MELANIE SHANKLE

SAN ANTONIO, TEXAS

It was sometime around Easter when it dawned on me that April was right around the corner, and I knew deep in my soul what was looming on the horizon.

So it was with fear and trembling that I opened Caroline's school bag the first week of April. Sure enough, there it was—the note announcing that San Antonio's annual Fiesta festival was coming around once again, and it was time to make shoebox floats for the Fiesta float parade at preschool.

Joy.

The note gives parents the option of just sending a shoebox to school and letting the teachers make a float for your child.

Right.

I wonder if they also offer some kind of complimentary therapy session for that poor kid? Hey, kid! Your mama doesn't love you enough to spend hours slaving away with a hot glue gun and some glitter mixed with sand to create the perfect beach scene for Ariel the Little Mermaid.

It's not like we have lives of our own. Lives that don't normally involve wielding a hot glue gun.

The note also included a little reminder that this is a preschool project and your child should be involved in the process.

Which is so nice—*in theory.*

So I involved Caroline by asking what kind of float she wanted to do and she answered without any hesitation, "Barbie Island Princess," which worked out nicely since we actually own Barbie Island Princess, along with her monkey, two little island girls, and an elephant named Sagi, who raised Barbie Island Princess from an infant when she was shipwrecked on a desert island, until she was finally rescued by Prince Antonio.

What has happened to my life?

Anyway, I managed to put the project in the back of my mind for the next few weeks because I am nothing if not a procrastinator. But I finally realized the due date was quickly approaching, so I headed to Michaels to pick up float-making supplies.

I loaded my basket with silk flowers, some greenery, glue sticks for my hot glue gun, and some bright Fiesta ribbon. While standing in line at the checkout, the woman in front of me looked at my basket and asked if I was making something for Fiesta. She was very perceptive.

When I replied that I was buying materials for my daughter's shoe-box float for school, she looked at me as if I had just announced that I was about to help my child cheat on the SATs. She said, "My kids had to do those when they were little. I just had them put a few stickers on a shoebox and called it a day."

Well, good for you, lady.

Clearly you are very healthy and have your priorities in order. Me? I happen to suffer from chronic OCD and the need to do simple craft projects in excess. It's who I am.

My reasoning is that there will come a day when Caroline will come home from school and ask for my help making a project for the science fair.

And she'll be out of luck.

Just the mention of the science fair makes me want to homeschool so that I can avoid all science-related homework. I know enough to teach Caroline that the Earth is flat and if she doesn't listen to her parents throughout her teen years there is a good chance she will fall off into the abyss. That's all the science she needs to know.

When I was in tenth grade, we were required to participate in the science fair, even though it was clear that some people—whose names don't need to be mentioned here—were having enough problems just memorizing the periodic table of elements without having to come up with some sort of hypothesis and conclusion.

(By the way, thank God I spent all that time memorizing the periodic table because it has been ever so useful in my adult life.)

I finally came up with an experiment that involved buying six goldfish with the goal of keeping three of them in total darkness and three of them in normal conditions and seeing which ones lived the longest. They all died within the week because I'm pretty sure I forgot to feed them due to the fact that I was busy deciding what to wear to the prom.

Thus, my science fair exhibit consisted of six empty fish bowls and a poster board that said, "I Murdered Six Goldfish Due to Negligence." And then PETA came and hauled my science teacher off to animal cruelty prison because he was an accessory to gold-fish murder.

Not really. But that would have been an awesome end to that story. The real story is that I got a C- on my project, which was basically a sympathy grade because the teacher knew I was scientifically impaired. The point is, I am much better with Barbie Island Princess floats and hot-gluing silk flowers.

Which is quite the marketable skill.

Caroline and I spent an afternoon pulling flowers off stems and deciding where to glue them on the shoebox. The biggest challenge was figuring out how to secure Barbie Island Princess to the float without hot-gluing her bottom directly onto it, because that seemed cruel. However, in the end, I had to hot glue her bottom directly to the float.

What do you expect? I hot glue Barbie bottoms and murder innocent goldfish.

I don't need to tell you that the float turned out so much better than my tenth-grade science fair project. At least, so I thought.

Until, at the parade, I saw a little girl whose float consisted of an electric horse that actually moved pulling a wagon made completely of Popsicle sticks painted hot pink with Western Barbie riding in the back.

I bet her mama got a D on her science fair project.

Melanie Shankle lives with her husband and daughter in San Antonio, Texas. She writes about her family's life at her blog, Big Mama (www. thebigmamablog.com). "In Memory of the Fish" was originally published on Melanie's blog as "In Somewhat Loving Memory of the Fish" (April 28, 2008) and adapted with permission. Melanie's first book,

Sparkly Green Earrings: Catching the Light at Every Turn, *was released in February 2013 by Tyndale House Publishers.*

5

MY SECOND CHANCE

JENNIFER SCOTT

ROME, GEORGIA

I will tell you what I know of my story, a mix of what I remember and what I've been told. Truly, it is God's mercy that I don't remember everything. It is only by his grace that I am here at all.

My husband and I were so excited when we found out we were expecting. We had had a hard time conceiving, as I had been diagnosed with polycystic ovarian syndrome, which meant that my body didn't ovulate properly. I chose to have hormone injections to encourage ovulation after other options failed.

One night before going out to dinner with friends, I took a pregnancy test, just so I would feel comfortable having a glass of wine if I wanted. And there it was—a line! It was faint, but a line nevertheless.

At six weeks, we went in for an ultrasound. My husband and I both watched the screen eagerly, and suddenly I cried out, "Two! I see two!" My husband, who is a doctor himself, agreed that we were looking at two babies.

Meanwhile, my ob/gyn continued with the scan. "Baby A measures such-and-such, Baby B, such-and-such," she said to the nurse. "Baby C measures . . ."

Baby C? Triplets! We laughed. We cried. We were in total shock.

Of course, carrying triplets creates a high-risk pregnancy. My doctor urged us to "selectively reduce" in order to lessen the risk. I knew what that term meant, and it was not an option for us.

I felt good throughout my pregnancy, but eventually I was put on bed rest at home. At 23 weeks, I went into labor and had to be hospitalized and given intravenous drugs to stop the contractions. I was in the hospital for eight and a half long weeks where I did nothing but eat, grow babies, and get big.

When I got to 31 weeks, the doctors decided to discontinue the drugs that were keeping my labor from progressing. They were concerned about my health, and at this point, the babies had developed enough to survive if I went into labor.

Sure enough, my contractions started within a few hours of stopping the drugs. In the early morning hours, I was wheeled into the operating room for a C-section. My babies—two boys and a girl—were delivered at 2 pounds, 6 ounces; 2 pounds, 12 ounces; and 3 pounds, 3 ounces. They were tiny but remarkably healthy; only one needed to be put on a breathing machine.

After recovery, I was wheeled back to my room, sleeping on and off, while my husband started calling people with the news. It got to be almost 8 o'clock and I was excited about *American Idol* coming on TV—the first season, Ryan Seacrest! I just couldn't seem to shake my grogginess, though. I assumed it was the pain medications, but things rapidly got worse.

"Honey, I can't get a good breath," I said, suddenly panicking. "It feels like there's an elephant on my chest."

My husband wasn't alarmed. *She just delivered three babies*, he thought. *Of course, she isn't feeling great.* But to humor me, he took out a stethoscope and listened to my heart and lungs. That's the last thing I remember.

My husband was shocked by what he heard. My lungs were filling up with fluid—he says it sounded as if I were drowning. And then foam started coming out of my mouth. He yelled for a nurse, who came in to check my blood oxygen levels. Alarmed, she called in a doctor, who ordered that I be taken for a chest X-ray.

But after years of dealing with critically ill patients, my husband realized that would be a fatal mistake. He could see that I was "coding"—going into full cardiac arrest. If I were taken to radiology, he knew I would probably die.

This wasn't my husband's hospital, so he was powerless to intervene. He ran out into the hall and over to an ob/gyn, who was sitting near the nurse's station.

"They're going to kill my wife! Don't let them take her to X-ray!" he shouted.

He begged the doctor to place me on a ventilator. Thankfully, the doctor agreed with my husband. The situation was so dire, they intubated me without even using anesthesia; they just shoved a tube down my throat. I was taken to ICU and started on drugs to halt my heart failure.

The next thing I remember is hearing my husband's voice. He was speaking in hushed tones. I didn't know where I was. I heard a woman crying. Someone was holding my hand, but I couldn't move. I thought, *Am I dead? Did I die?*

I didn't know they had given me paralytic drugs in the recovery room to keep me from pulling out my tubes. I tried with all my might to squeeze the hand holding mine, and then I recognized my mother's voice.

"She just squeezed my hand!" she cried. The effort was so great that I immediately blacked out again.

For the next thirty-six hours I slipped in and out of consciousness. My heart wasn't pumping well. In fact, only a third of patients in my condition recover fully. One-third of patients die and the other third live, but with severe disabilities. No one could predict which group I would be in. They discussed whether a heart transplant might be necessary.

My medications began to work, though, and I became more conscious with each passing day. Even in my weakened condition, it weighed on me that I hadn't seen my babies yet. My husband showed me photos—they looked like little baby squirrels!—but their lives were starting and I wasn't a part of it. To feel so disconnected from the lives I had fought so hard to protect was an agony worse than any physical pain.

Little did I know that a covert operation was underway. One night at midnight, a nurse came down the hallway rolling an isolette. She had my babies! My husband arranged a blanket over me, and the nurse laid the babies down on my chest one by one. They were wearing bibs that covered their entire bodies and crocheted booties and caps that their great-grandmother had made for them.

I was so excited to see them and to touch them! The babies were groggy but moving around a little. I examined every inch of them—their eyes, their ears, their hair, their fingers and toes. From their appearance, to their sounds and their smells, I marveled at all the miraculous little things new parents coo about when they see their babies for the first time.

We didn't know it then, but I wasn't out of the woods by a long shot. A few days later, I came down with pneumonia and a highly contagious bacterial infection that forced me into isolation. I wasn't allowed any visitors at all, certainly not the babies. Even my doctors had to gown and glove themselves to come into my room. I was in the hospital for nine weeks total before I was well enough to go home. It felt like an all-out assault on my life.

But for those brief moments in my hospital room, cuddled up with my precious babies, I was content. I felt peaceful and my racing heart slowed. Seeing them, touching them, our little family of five together at last, I felt for the first time that things were going to be okay.

To this day, eight years later, my heart doesn't work at full capacity and I am on medication for life. Yet, I strive to live each day with the awareness that I could have missed out on all of it. Life is short, and not everybody gets a second chance. I got that chance, and I am so grateful that God allowed me to stick around to enjoy the miraculous roles of wife and mother.

Jennifer Scott lives in Rome, Georgia, with her husband, Ryland, and their three children. Before the birth of her triplets, she was a recruiter and management trainer for a financial services company. She blogs from the trenches of motherhood at Lots of Scotts (www.lotsofscotts.blogspot.com).

6

AN ANGEL IN MY POCKET

BRENDA KUCZMA UNDERWOOD

SPRINGFIELD, ILLINOIS

Believers, look up—take courage.
The angels are nearer than you think.

BILLY GRAHAM

My husband, Steve, came home from work one night and excitedly announced that he had gotten a job promotion. I threw my arms around him, thrilled that he had achieved this long-sought goal.

My bubble of happiness, however, didn't last long.

"We would have to move to another city," he added.

My arms dropped away from him.

"Move? But we can't move right now!" I protested. "Beth is only in fourth grade. And Bryan has to finish eighth grade and graduate in May. Plus, I have to complete my nursing degree and graduate in May as well. Oh, and did you forget that Bryan wants to get his Eagle Scout project done by May, too?"

My head swam. I couldn't believe this was happening.

"I've already worked that out with the company," Steve told me gently. "We don't have to move until the summer. However, I will have to begin working in Springfield before you and Bryan graduate."

This news left me numb. He'd be working in a different city, and I would be left behind to play single mom. *God, can you make this any more difficult?* I screamed in my head.

As if returning to nursing school at age 40 and as a mother with two kids wasn't hard enough, I would now have to do it all on my own. How could something as great as a job promotion sound so . . . *bad?*

I tried to dismiss my selfish thoughts, but the reality of it was that this brand of solo parenting felt nearly impossible. My mind raced with thoughts of all the things I would have to do alone: study and finish nursing school, help the kids with homework and drive them to their activities, plus attend all of their special events—piano recitals, band concerts, school fundraisers, sports banquets, and end-of-the-year events. Then, there was Bryan's Eagle Scout project and badge. I caught Steve's eye.

"We'll have to look at houses in Springfield on the weekends," he told me. "Plus, we'll have to sell our house in the meantime."

I plopped down on a chair and sighed heavily. My heart went into overdrive and my anxiety level shot to the ceiling. Tears started streaming down my face.

Okay, God, I'm going to need some help down here, I pleaded silently. I repeated an old saying to myself—"What God brings you to, He takes you through"—but still I added a postscript to my prayer.

God, you better send me plenty of angel support—a whole truckload of it!

Steve reached down and put his arms around me. "Brenda, you can do this. No, *we* can do this! It will be a challenge, but somehow we'll manage. One day at a time," he said.

Suddenly, I realized that this would be my secret to handling everything in the next five months. I would never look too far down the road and do only what I needed to do, one day at a time. With that new thought, my anxiety and stress dropped from a Level 10 down to at least a Level 5.

Thereafter, I was up at 5 o'clock every morning on the treadmill with my nursing notes propped up in front of me. Next, I got the kids up, let the dog out, made breakfast for all, straightened the rooms for house showings, and glanced through the schedule of after-school activities for the day. When I felt overwhelmed, I told myself, *Brenda, take a deep breath and remember: One day at a time!*

Every morning I'd pray for help to get through the day and to do the best I could as a student, a mom, and a wife. At night, as I fell into bed, I would thank God for getting me through the day and ask his help for the next day.

One day, I bought a coin with a hologram of an angel on it, which I began to slip into my nursing uniform pocket every day. That little token was my constant reminder that I wasn't really alone in all this. *Right, God?* I'd think to myself. "*Fear not, I am always with you," and all that stuff? I sure hope so!*

As the months accelerated, so did my confidence. Yet the dreaded month of May was fast approaching. End-of-the-year school activities crowded our schedule and my obligations as a mother started to mount, especially with Bryan's middle school graduation coming up.

But the worst part for me was the last nursing clinical rotation before my own graduation. It was the most difficult rotation of all and a requirement to graduate—the "make it or break it" rotation. It was also the one with the toughest and most intimidating instructor.

On the day of the rotation, I spoke aloud to myself, "Brenda, take hold of yourself. Remember, one day at a time. I *will* get through this and I *will* graduate." All I had to do now was believe what I'd just said.

Sliding my hand into the pocket of my nursing uniform, I felt my coin. *Okay, angel,* I thought to myself, *do your thing.*

The final rotation included the most difficult nursing skill—starting an IV. Until this point, we had only practiced with a computerized program. Now it was time to demonstrate this skill on an actual patient with an instructor hovering over us.

My instructor, the toughest of them all, was loud, strict, and showed no mercy. Standing next to me, she barked out orders to gather the IV materials, and my hands began to shake.

I glanced down at the patient lying in the hospital bed and froze. I would have to find a vein, stick the needle in, and hope to see the blood coming through the tubing. Getting it right the first time meant success. A second try meant failure from this instructor.

As I searched the arm of the patient for a good vein, a nursing student ran into the room, and in a stressed voice told the instructor she was needed elsewhere. "Watch this student do the IV procedure and report back to me!" the instructor barked to a staff nurse in the hall as she left the room.

I couldn't believe my ears or my luck. Instead of having the merciless instructor breathing down my neck, this pretty young blonde nurse would observe me. I felt the angel coin in my pocket and told myself I could do this.

With shaking hands and a wildly racing heart, I silently prayed, *Oh God, if ever I need you, it's now!*

A hand gently touched my arm. "Brenda," the staff nurse told me quietly, "you can do this."

A strange, yet peaceful feeling came over me. I looked down at the patient's arm, found a good vein, and slid the needle in. Blood sprang up through the tube. Success! The nurse squeezed my arm and smiled. She wrote the report for my instructor as I cleaned up the materials. When I was finished, she was gone.

Wanting to thank her, I went out to the hallway to find her. I didn't know her name, and I couldn't remember seeing a name tag.

I went to the nurses' station and asked about the pretty blonde nurse. The staff nurses looked at each other in confusion. "Ha! Sorry, honey! We don't have any cute blondes here, just us old brunettes!" one of them told me with a laugh.

Puzzled, I slowly walked away. Who was that nurse who helped guide me? I felt that now-familiar peaceful feeling again. Smiling to myself, I slipped my hand into my uniform pocket and found my angel coin. "Thank you, God," I whispered. He had answered the prayers of an overwhelmed mom after all.

Brenda Kuczma Underwood is a registered nurse who lives in Springfield, Illinois, where she is wellness director for the Healthy Heart program at a health club facility. She and her husband, Steve, have two children, Bryan and Beth. Initially earning her degree in psychology, Brenda returned to college later in life to pursue her dream of becoming a nurse. "An Angel in My Pocket" first appeared on the website Faith, Hope and Fiction (www.faithhopeandfiction.com) and is reprinted and adapted with the author's permission.

7

SONGS OF A MOTHER'S HEART

BROOK LEGG
GULF COAST, MISSISSIPPI

Music is well said to be the speech of angels.

THOMAS CARLYLE

When my son Joshua was about 2 years old, I made up a song called the "Hold You" song. It goes like this:

Hold you, I love to hold you, my little boy
Hold you, I love to hold you, my little boy
Hold you, I love to hold you, my little boy
My little boy, I love to hold you.

I know—really creative, right? But I've found that songs can be powerful, no matter what the words.

I never thought I'd be a mom at all. I never really thought about it growing up. We moved around a lot, and I was raised as an only child; my brother lived with my dad.

On top of that, I had the usual pressures of school. In Texas, cheerleading is a big deal. I was a cheerleader for many years, even though I was a little on the heavy side. A boy in school once said, within my hearing, "Brook is so cute. If only she'd lose 20 pounds." I was crushed.

My way of dealing with the hurts of my childhood was destructive. I decided to take control of my life through food, and eventually, I became anorexic. I'm 5-foot-3, and at one point, I weighed just 98 pounds.

We moved the summer between my sophomore and junior years, and I was home by myself most of the time, in an apartment in a new town, with no real schedule. I fell into binging and purging and my anorexia turned into bulimia. In my junior year of high school, I confided to my brother about my struggle. It was a cry for help, I think. He told my mother, and I got help for the first time, a month of outpatient treatment.

But the activities of my senior year were all about body image and looks. I was cheerleading again, and participating in the homecoming court. At one point, I went to live with my aunt. My anorexia and bulimia had returned and were so bad I was taking laxatives and vomiting every day. I would turn on the shower so my aunt wouldn't hear me.

One day, I was in such terrible shape that I couldn't even stay in class. I called my mom and said to her, "If I don't get help, I'm going to die." My mom was always there for me when I needed help. She got me into treatment again, this time in a residential program. I was able to graduate from high school on time by taking adult classes at a nearby college.

After high school, I joined the Navy. I continued to struggle with eating issues, but I was able to do my job at staff command in New Orleans. At my church, I met a woman who took me under her wing.

She was a homeschooling mom who showed me by example what it was to be a godly woman. I had always been a believer, but because of her, my relationship with God grew stronger during my time in the Navy.

After I left the military, a man I had worked with in the Navy contacted a friend of mine and asked her to pass along a message. "Please tell her that I like her," he requested. Steve was a believer who wanted to help me fulfill my desire to be a godly wife and mother. Within four months we were married!

But Steve was still in the military, and so again I was alone a lot. I felt the pull of my eating disorder once again. I desperately wanted to be free of it, but I still felt like I was in bondage. One day, Steve went out of town, and my immediate response was to head to the kitchen.

Standing in front of the pantry, I cried out, "Am I never going to be rid of this, God? I know you can set me free! Why won't you set me free?"

In that moment, I felt God's spirit speak to my spirit. *You know I'm here*, he said. *Sing to me.* So I started to sing a worship song. I don't even remember what the song was; I can't recall the words. But singing that song of praise gave me the strength to shut the pantry door.

I went into our bedroom and lay down on the bed and cried. But my tears were tears of relief and joy. *I had the power through Christ to choose victory!* The words of a song had set me free.

It was in a moment of frustration again years later, after I had had our first child, that my soul sang again. The first time I sang the "Hold You" song, it was Joshua's naptime, but he wouldn't go to sleep. He was a wiggle worm without the least interest in napping. *How will I ever get him to close his eyes?* I thought in desperation.

That's when I pulled him close and sang the simple words of my made-up song. A peacefulness came over him and his eyes started to close. From then on, sharing the song with him became our nap-time ritual.

I have had many precious moments singing the "Hold You" song to my son over the years. Now that he is eight, I'm afraid he is almost too old for it, but he still lets me sing it to him from time to time. My daughters, who are five and two, are beginning to say, "Mommy, will you sing the 'Hold You' song for me?"

The other day, I was in my laundry room, where I change my babies' diapers, and I drew my 2-year-old into my arms for a snuggle. Inspiration hit me once again and I sang her these words:

Who's the little baby?

Baby that I love.

Who's the precious gift from God sent from up above?

Ellie is her name

Ellie is her name

Ellie Lynn is her name.

My baby looked into my eyes, and we shared a moment of sweet connection. I think this song is going to be another big hit in my mommy repertoire.

Brook Legg and her husband, Steve, live on Mississippi's Gulf Coast, where they are raising four children, Joshua, Abigail, Ellie, and Anna. Brook writes poetry and worship songs, and her husband plays drums for their church's worship team. She has published The Healing Rhythms of Home *(WestBow, 2012), a book of devotions for homeschooling moms, and is working on a children's book about a polar bear who learns how to love.*

8

It's Just Hair

DEBBY MENDELSOHN
CLAREMONT, CALIFORNIA

My son Doug always had a thing about his hair. Even as a little guy, he liked to mess around with his hair. He had gorgeous golden locks, with natural highlights that people pay hairdressers hundreds of dollars for.

Doug moussed his hair and spiked it with gel. He'd ask for a military cut like the soldiers he so admired, or to have designs cut into his hair, like his African American friend Tevan's hair. He liked his Hispanic friend Jèsus's hair and was disappointed when he couldn't style his straight, blond hair in the same way.

All in all, although Doug had fun with his hair, it was something he took very seriously.

He couldn't pass a mirror or window without checking it and fixing it to his liking. His hair was nothing less than an outward expression of who he was.

One day, when Doug was 9 years old and in the fourth grade, we were talking at home about a friend's child, a girl who was very sick with cancer. The girl's parents were close friends of mine from college, so their daughter's sickness was devastating for me.

Little Sammy was just 8 years old when she was diagnosed with rhabdomyosarcoma, an aggressive soft-tissue tumor that most often strikes children. Sammy was such a sweet little girl—happy, outgoing, a cheerleader. Her nickname was Sammy Salsa, because she was such an energetic and spunky little person.

Sammy had to endure so much. She was undergoing aggressive chemotherapy and radiation treatments, and suffering all the pain and nausea and complications they bring. These were dark days for our dear friends.

My kids had never known anyone who was this sick, and so Doug and his sister had a lot of questions. That day, I had gotten a call from my friend, who told me that Sammy's hair was falling out because of the chemo treatments. Sammy had been a brunette with shiny, flowing hair that fell to her shoulders.

When my son and daughter got home from school, they could see how upset I was. I explained to them that Sammy's treatment was like a poison to her body, including her hair, and that one of the side effects was that she was going to be entirely bald.

"But, Mom, I don't see the problem," Doug protested. "It's just hair."

Spoken like a true boy! So, I told them how hard it can be for sick children—especially girls—to lose their hair. Sammy loved to brush and style her hair, put it into ponytails and tie it with ribbons. For Sammy, to have her hair fall out was like losing her identity. It was a constant reminder that she was sick.

Later that day, Doug came into the kitchen to talk with me.

"Mom, I want Sammy to feel better about losing her hair," he said. "I want to show her that she's not the only one who's going to be bald—I want to shave my head."

Doug must have seen a hint of horror in my face, because he jumped right in with assurances.

"Mom, I won't be bald forever. It'll grow back," he said. "It's just hair."

In those few seconds after his pronouncement, my mind had raced through a million different thoughts. *What will people think? Will they think he has cancer? Will kids at school tease him? He absolutely loves his hair—won't he regret this impulsive decision?*

But ultimately, my mind settled on one single thought: I was so proud of my son. My mother's heart soared when I considered his desire to do such a loving and generous thing. And Doug's words rang in my ears: *It's just hair.*

So, we got out the cape and hair clippers, walked out to the patio and went to work. Even though my husband is in the Army National Guard and I had cut his hair many times, I didn't really know what I was doing. My hand was shaking when I picked up the clippers.

I felt such conflicting emotions as I began. With each pass of the clippers, I saw Doug's thick, blond hair fall in clumps to the ground. It was so much harder than I thought it would be. But I was spurred on by the thought that for Doug, going bald was a choice, while for Sammy it was not. It was her hard reality.

We made an afternoon of it. Doug decided he wanted to make an album for Sammy, so we got out a camera, and my daughter Mel took pictures as we went along. Using colored gel, we spiked splotches of unshaven hair into funny shapes, and Doug posed for crazy photos. I cut all the hair from the top first, leaving him looking like a balding, middle-aged man with a ring of hair around his head. We laughed all afternoon long, as we gradually filled a baggie with his shaven, golden locks.

When we were finished, Doug grabbed a mirror, eager to see the end result. He grinned from ear to ear as he rubbed his bowling-ball head and then laughed at how smooth it felt.

"Wait 'til Sammy sees this!" he cried.

This was a magical moment for me. When I looked at my Doug, I didn't see a shockingly bald child—I just saw the most beautiful little boy in the entire world.

"I am so proud of you! You are so handsome!" I said to him. And I meant it.

The whole experience left me feeling very blessed. I was so grateful to have healthy children, and to have the kind of loving children who could show such great empathy for others.

I had to hold onto that thought, because later that night, rummaging around in Doug's backpack, I pulled out a rumpled sheet of paper from the very bottom. Unfolding it, I saw that it was an order form . . . for next week's school picture day!

My heart did a quick flip, but then I started to laugh. After all, I shrugged—it's just hair!

Debby Mendelsohn owns a public relations consulting business in Southern California, where she specializes in environmental legislative issues and governmental affairs. She writes for local and national magazines on a variety of topics and volunteers as a Family Readiness Group leader for the California Army National Guard; in 2012, she and her family were recognized as Volunteer Family of the Year by the Association of the United States Army. Debby gives thanks every day for the many blessings in her life, including her husband, Bill, and their children, Doug and Mel. She delights in sharing sporting, musical, theatrical, and spiritual adventures with her family.

NOTE: Today, five years after treatment, Sammy is cancer free. She participated in the Miss America scholarship program and was a national spokesperson for Hyundai's Hope on Wheels campaign, which raises money for pediatric cancer research. She is a Wish Ambassador and speaks to groups about the Make-A-Wish Foundation, the popular charitable organization that grants wishes for children with life-threatening medical conditions. "Debby's kids are awesome!" Sammy's mother, Erin Heim, says. "We have been so blessed by all the support, love, and prayers of our family and friends."

9

If Only I Spoke Bug

GINGER LYONS

SPOKANE, WASHINGTON

"You're my best friend. I wuv you!"

This declaration of love came from my 2-year-old son, Dylan. The object of his affection? Not me, but a caterpillar.

For more than an hour, Dylan had been playing with the fuzzy little caterpillar in his great-grandparents' backyard. Thanks to Dylan, the caterpillar was now doing things that it had never—and I'm just guessing here—done before. He had learned to crawl up a very dirty little boy's toes and survived a trip sailing through the air. He had attempted to eat a gummy worm and had even played a rousing game of "Ring Around the Rosie."

Anticipating a teaching moment and feeling a sense of parental obligation, my husband explained to Dylan that this lowly little caterpillar would one day become a beautiful butterfly, and after that he would be able to fly and do all kinds of exciting things.

Dylan stared at the greenish-brown critter as it inched its way across his hand.

"But he's beautiful now, daddy," he said. "And he can fly already—WATCH!"

Once again, the fuzzy creature went sailing through the air.

Dylan and the caterpillar lay contentedly side by side on the concrete patio with the sun's rays beating down on them, blissfully unaware of the sudden shadow falling over them. An instant later, the caterpillar was squashed and Dylan's big brother—the bottom of his shoe to be precise—was the assailant. It was a brutal scene.

"Call the ambulance!" Dylan screamed, while his big brother protested loudly, "It was an accident!"

In the midst of the mayhem, Daddy grabbed a tissue and respectfully removed the carcass from the scene.

As I comforted both boys and attempted to prevent another untimely death, I thought of the caterpillar's mother. If I spoke bug, I would tell her what I learned from my son and hers that day: *We're beautiful now!*

With his innocent observation, Dylan had taken my breath away. After thirty-two years on earth, I needed my two-year-old to explain the meaning of life to me. I'm constantly worrying about the future— where I will go, what I will do, what my children will do, what they will become. But God is happy with us *now*. He thinks we're beautiful *now*.

Yes, if I were able, I would tell that caterpillar mama that her gentle offspring was well-loved up to the final moment of his life, and that he did not die in vain. I would tell her of the life-changing lesson I learned from my son and his fuzzy little companion that day.

I comforted Dylan on the loss of his best friend for well over three minutes as his tears fell. But then he lifted his head and spotted something out of the corner of his eye.

"Come here, buggy!" Dylan shrieked at an innocent little click beetle. I sighed and sent up a prayer for the beetle mom.

Ginger Lyons and her husband, Lance, live in Spokane, Washington, and have two boys, Colton and Dylan. She is an entrepreneur who started and sold a specialty food company. In addition to writing, Ginger repurposes vintage jewelry though her business, Peace, Love & Pearls, and is co-owner of a home décor company, Buffalo Girls Vintage, both of which can be found on Facebook.

10

MOSIE'S MOM

BRENDA NIXON

MOUNT VERNON, OHIO

I met Mosie when he was 19 years old. My daughter's church youth group was planning a mission trip to Nicaragua, and the group was looking for odd jobs to earn its way. We had some trees we said they could fell and haul away.

One Saturday, four muscled young men showed up at our door. They were an unusual work crew—all of them had recently left their Amish families and were out on their own. Their transition into our society had not been happy or easy.

We live near the country's largest number of Amish settle-ments. Around here, most Amish belong to the Old Order Amish or the Swartzentruber Amish, which is the strictest, most punitive Amish order.

In these communities, everything—everything!—is dictated to you. How to cut your hair, the width of your hat brim, whether your clothing has buttons, hooks, or safety pins, the shape of the eyelets on your shoes, the height of your shoe soles, the color of your socks, the number of pleats in an apron—even the undergarments you have to

wear. The church decides the décor of your home and the design of
your buggy, and tells you what food to bring to a church social. You
are taught from an early age that strict obedience to these rules is the
way of righteousness.

Children who grow up in the Swartzentruber Amish are sheltered,
naïve about things of the world, childlike in their demeanor even as
teens. Most are kind people, honest, and diligent workers. But they
can be emotionally stunted. Parents don't hug their children or touch
them in any affectionate way, believing it will make their children
prideful. Children never hear an encouraging comment like "That's
a great idea" or "I'm proud of you." The slightest nonconformity
or disobedience on a child's part results in a whipping or in public
church discipline.

Many teens rebel against this rigid and arid upbringing. If they
do, they have no choice but to leave their families. When they slip out,
they're painfully cut off from their families, the church, and everything they've ever known. Their families consider that these children
have been turned over to Satan with no hope of heaven unless they
return and repent.

The day the boys came over to our house, my daughter pointed to
one and said quietly, "Do you see that boy over there, Mom? That's
Mosie. His parents don't want him anymore."

Mosie had left his farm in a Swartzentruber community in upstate
New York about ten months earlier. He had made his way to Ohio to
join some friends and cousins who had also left. He slipped out in the
middle of the night with only fifty dollars and the clothes on his back.

At one point, Mosie went back to his farm on a Sunday morning
when he knew his family would be at church. He searched quickly
through the house for his birth certificate, which he needed to start

his new life. Although he found the documents for each of his eleven siblings, his was missing. He believed his father had taken it.

Months later, lonely and desperately homesick, Mosie went to New York again hoping to see his family. He knocked on the door of the farmhouse but got no response. He saw the curtains at a window move, but no one came to the door.

When I heard Mosie's story, my mother's heart broke wide open.

"Well," I said to my daughter, "if Mosie's parents don't want him, then we do. I'll be his English mom."

As we got to know Mosie over the next few weeks, we talked it over with our daughters, and we prayed about "adopting" him into our family. Although we couldn't legally adopt Mosie, we could sign paperwork drawn up especially for so-called English who want to take in Amish runaways.

One day, our daughter approached Mosie with my idea.

"My mom and dad want to adopt you," she said. "What do you think?"

Mosie thought about it and responded quietly, "I would like that."

And so in November, on his twentieth birthday, Mosie came to our house for an adoption ceremony. We all signed the commitment document, and I framed a copy of it and hung it in our kitchen. We became Mosie's English parents.

Mosie lived with us for a year while we helped him get a job, open a bank account, buy a used car, do his income taxes, wrestle with insurance—all the things we had done for our own children. We got him haircuts, an eye exam, went shopping for clothes, and took him to his first real dentist appointment. I taught Mosie things that are standard in our society but not in his—how to brush his teeth, how to say please and thank you, how to show and accept affection. We helped him with the English language, because the German dialect of the Amish was his first language. When the need arose, we corrected him as we had our own children, and we celebrated his successes.

Mosie is smart and quick-witted. He grew so much in so short a time. He started on his GED and found work on a horse farm, which he says is his dream job. He has accepted Christ as his Savior, and we have been privileged to show him that our God is a loving God who wants the best for him, not a penalizing God who is looking to crush him at any moment for breaking a rule. We are as proud of him as we are of our two daughters.

In time, my husband and I encouraged Mosie to move out on his own, to start an independent adult life. But he still comes home to us, and he joins us on family vacations. He calls me Mama and lets me hug him—simple expressions of love that, until now, he has never known. We still pray that Mosie's family will open their hearts to receive him again. But no matter what happens, Mosie will always be our son. We will always love him.

Brenda Nixon, MA, is a popular speaker and host of the internet radio show The Parent's Plate *(www.toginet.com/shows/theparentsplate). She has authored the award-winning* The Birth to Five Book *(Revell, 2009), co-authored* A Scrapbook of Christmas Firsts *(Leafwood, 2008), and has contributed to thirty titles, including several in the Chicken Soup for the Soul series. She is at work on a nonfiction book about former Amish children. In addition to their adopted son, Brenda and her husband have two adult children, including a daughter who is married to another former Amish.*

11

A MIRACLE MOMENT

NIKKI KENDALL

OMAHA, NEBRASKA

Today was a very difficult day for me. Today marked the second anniversary of the death of our son, Eric.

My husband and I lost Eric when he was only 15 months old. He suffered from what the doctors called a "mystery diagnosis."

Eric was only four days old when he had his first surgery for a bowel blockage. After that, he never really got well. He underwent test after test, but the doctors didn't really know why he was failing. They guessed it might be his immune system attacking his body.

Eric's treatment was similar to that of children who are fighting cancer: chemotherapy, immune suppressive therapy, and a bone marrow transplant. Dave and I lived with our other son in a hotel next to the children's hospital for ten months while Eric was being treated.

It is hard to hand over your child to complete strangers, even when you know they are charged with caring for him. You give up so much control in a hospital. It is a hard pill to swallow, realizing that you can do absolutely nothing to help your child.

We had many close calls during those ten months, but over time Eric seemed to get better. The doctors were preparing to move him from the intensive care unit to the regular bone marrow transplant floor. But on the day of his discharge from the ICU, he unexpectedly lost his fight. He died on October 1, 2009.

After Eric died, I took up running for Team in Training to benefit the Leukemia and Lymphoma Society. It was such a huge relief to be among people who understood our grief, because they'd been through it, too.

Today, two years later, I participated with my team in a practice run for the Nike Marathon.

It is hard to run when your throat is tight from holding back tears. But I managed to finish the ten miles of the run. I was heading down to our post-run gathering by the lake when a teammate hopped out of her car.

Beth is eight months pregnant, so she isn't training this season. Still, she stopped by to support her teammates. She approached me a little tentatively.

"Nikki, I know this is going to sound weird," she said, "But a week or so ago I woke up at 2 A.M., thinking about you. I know that you lost your son sometime in October, and I had this strong feeling that you were going to need something today. So I brought you this . . ."

Saying this, Beth handed me three balloons, stationery, and a pen.

"I thought you could write a letter to your son and then send it up to him," she said.

When she said this, I just started to cry. I told her that today was the actual anniversary of our loss, and then she started to cry. She hugged me tight, even though she was big with her pregnancy and I was a sweaty mess from running.

It took me a good twenty minutes to recover, and then Beth helped me write out my note and connect it to the balloons. Beth's son, Cael, helped me release the balloons, and together we stood and watched them float away over the lake.

Over these past two years, I have heard many stories like mine—stories of miraculous moments when a grieving person receives the comfort they need just when they need it. Today was my miracle moment.

A moment like this keeps me running for the cause. I run for every mom who has had to see her baby endure chemo. I run for every mom who has had to wear a paper hospital gown just to touch her baby. I run for every mom who never got to bring her baby home. I run in memory of my son, Eric.

Nikki Kendall was a social worker for a child protection services agency, but after the death of her son, she founded Kendall Personal Fitness and became a personal trainer. She participates in marathons and half marathons for the Leukemia and Lymphoma Society's Team in Training, which raises funds for cancer patients and their families. She and her husband, Dave, live in Omaha, Nebraska, with their son, Wes. She blogs at Mom on a Mission (www.nikkiisamomonamission.blogspot.com).

12

THE DAY THE SHOE DROPPED

NORA PEACOCK

NEWBERG, OREGON

"Mom, are you sitting down?"

My heart dropped to my stomach as I answered the phone call from my son, Larry. Until the proverbial other shoe drops, these words make a parent stop breathing. All sorts of possibilities flooded my mind.

Maybe he's getting married. Yes! That's it. He's calling to announce the big news!

He hasn't broken a leg, has he? When will this kid quit trying to become the next great basketball star?

I know, he's moving to some faraway state to stake his claim to fame. Maybe I'll see him once a year . . . if I'm lucky.

Okay, time to pry my fingers off. Larry's a big boy. I need to let him spread his wings and fly.

"Mom. . . . Mom, are you there?"

My fingers clutched the phone while I cleared my throat. "Umm . . . yeah, I'm sitting down."

His voice sounds strong. Good. At least he's not dying. *Is he?*

Time to get a grip, to halt my mental train that's fast hurtling off a cliff.

"So, what's up?" I asked, lightly. Just call me "Ms. Casual."

"I've signed on the dotted line."

What dotted line? I know. He's buying that four-wheel-drive truck he's always wanted. Maybe even a house. A big decision, but . . .

"Mom, I joined the Army."

My heart skipped a beat—no, it skipped several beats.

"What? Say that again?"

"I've joined the Army National Guard."

My breathing restarted. The National Guard. That's not so bad. He can clean up flooded cities, hurricane and tornado disaster zones, and . . .

Wait a minute. Gone are the good old days when the National Guard stays stateside.

I forced my wandering thoughts back to my son's confident voice.

"I've always wanted to serve my country," Larry said. "With the economy the way it is, I can't get steady work. This just seems like the right time to go for it."

But . . . can't someone else's son wear camo? Can't someone else's son crawl on his stomach through a swamp? Someone else's son hunker down in a trench, bullets zipping over his head?

Take a deep breath, Mom. He isn't there—yet.

Maybe he'll sit behind some office desk pushing papers for Uncle Sam. Maybe he'll never leave the U.S. of A. Maybe . . .

"Wow, Larry. So, are you sure about this?" I asked.

The glimmer of patriotic pride in my boy's voice edged its way into my consciousness, and I heard a burst of nervous laughter.

What? Did I say something funny? What did I just miss?

"Too late now. It's a done deal." Larry's chatter stopped, as if he was waiting for my vote of confidence.

Okay. Back to the safe desk job. Who was I to rain on his parade? No more waxing eloquent about "my little boy." I struggled to calm my voice.

"So, Mr. Soldier Man, are you going to play your trombone for the Army band?" I asked, still hoping for an out.

Yes, that sounds safe. After all, in his senior year of high school, my pride-and-joy had written a whole symphony that the school band had played at graduation.

"Nope. I want to get some training that I can use when I get out," he said, snuffing out that possibility.

So, join some orchestra. Or show them your genius as an artist. Yeah, that's the ticket. Strut your stuff, my son of many talents. Surely the Army could use a good artist.

"How about drafting? Maybe they need somebody to design bridges or . . ."

"I applied for that. There aren't any slots right now in that career field."

My mother's intuition told me that the size 15 shoe was about to drop with a thud.

"I'm going to be a medic, Mom. A combat medic," Larry said.

I squeezed my eyes shut and swallowed the lump in my throat.

"That's . . . that's really . . ."

"Think about it, Mom. There are always jobs in the medical field." His voice picked up speed. "When I get out, I'll be able to work wherever I want to live."

He was right. But so what! He had to live to tell about it first! Just a minor detail.

My mouth went dry. I clutched a wad of my shirt over my heart. Images of snarling drill sergeants slapped my senses. How can I release my precious child to the harsh arms of boot camp, much less to some gritty battlefield where death surrounds him? And what if—I can barely finish this thought—*what if some day he comes home in a casket?*

I struggled as I tried to force my grim thoughts to settle down.

After that heart-stopping call, the weeks passed all too quickly as Larry prepared to mark his rite of passage from civilian to soldier, from the freedom of coming and going as he pleases to the reality of Uncle Sam ordering every minute of his every day.

At the end of one particularly emotional day, I sat by the very phone that had dared to rock my world, my Bible in my lap. My mind was flooded with memories of Larry's childhood, and I struggled yet again to come to terms with his very adult decision.

So I hadn't quite let go of the "little boy" stuff yet. Helplessness overwhelmed me once again as I wiped away my tears.

Before Larry boards that huge gray plane that will carry him away, what words of wisdom could I possibly choose for my soldier boy? What pillar of truth will sustain this child of my womb in the years ahead, when he may risk his life so that I and others might live in freedom? Beyond the love I have for him and the prayers I offer up continually for him, what guidance might I offer that could possibly make a difference in his hour of need? In *my* hour of need.

I flipped to the concordance in the back of my Bible. Strength. Yes, something about strength. My finger scanned the pages until I found the word "strong."

"My son, be strong, in the grace that is in Christ Jesus." I see these words in 2 Timothy 2:1.

There they were. The words I needed.

Hope and assurance stilled my anxious heart. "Oh, Lord Jesus, thank you," I prayed. "As Larry marches on into his future, I know you will be there for him. I release my soldier boy into your loving care. I am confident you have good plans for Larry's life, no matter what the future holds."

Be strong, my son. God's love and my love go with you.

Nora Peacock is a freelance writer who lives in Newberg, Oregon. Her articles, stories, and poetry have been published in the Christian Communicator, *the* Oregon Christian Writers *newsletter,* Northwest Senior Boomer & News, LIVE, the Secret Place, *and Gary Chapman's books,* Love Is a Verb *(Bethany House, 2010) and* Love Is a Verb Devotional *(Bethany House, 2011). She and her husband, Arlen, are the parents of seven adult children and the grandparents of eight grandchildren.*

13

A NEW MOM

LEAH GONZALEZ
JACKSONVILLE, NORTH CAROLINA

Though no one can go back and make a brand new start,
anyone can start from now and make a brand new ending.

UNKNOWN

Yesterday, I put on a new dress to wear to church. It ended mid-knee, which is shorter than the dresses I usually wear, and I was worried about my white legs showing so much.

As I finished getting ready, my 11-year-old son walked into the bedroom and stopped to look at me.

"Mom, that dress makes you look weird," Alex said.

"Weird? Weird, like how?" I asked, thinking he'd say something about my pasty white legs or my knees.

"I dunno," he answered. "Weird . . . like . . . skinny."

I laughed as I absorbed my son's words. These days, I'll take that kind of compliment!

Over the last few years, I've been on a weight loss journey. I've lost 66 pounds so far, and I'm on target to reach my goal weight of 140 pounds—90 pounds lighter than when I started.

Alex was only 2 years old when he last saw me looking the way I do now, so of course he doesn't remember me the way I was. Until a few years ago, the mom that he and his two sisters knew weighed 232 pounds and was rapidly outgrowing her size 20W clothes.

I had pretty much resigned myself to the fact that I was the fat mom. I didn't like it, but I'm an outgoing person and I tried not to let it bother me. I was content to be the mom who sat on the sidelines and cheered for her kids, not the mom who went on walks or rode bikes with her kids.

It was a natural role for me. I grew up in a family that valued music and books. Sports and the active life weren't something I aspired to. Besides, my husband filled that role—he grew up in Mexico playing soccer until the sun went down, and he ran track and played other sports after he came to the States as a teen. He was also fit because of his career with the Navy. He was the one who took our kids outside to shoot hoops or play in the yard. I didn't have either the energy or the desire to join them.

Although my kids didn't complain, the extent of my motherhood was pretty limited. I was there to bake cookies for them and get them where they needed to go, and that was it.

I tried to be content with my size. It didn't stop me from volunteering at my kids' school, although when I came in to help with my son's reading group, I realized with a shock how far away from the table I had to sit. But on the inside, I was constantly comparing myself to the other moms. I always noticed how cute they looked and thought sadly to myself, *That won't ever be me.*

One day, I pulled out a box of size 14 clothing that I had saved, hoping I'd fit into it again some day. Wanting to gain some self-acceptance and peace, I threw out the clothes, and immediately I felt a sense of freedom from my expectations.

Then I went out and gained another 10 pounds.

I started to have trouble with my knees. I couldn't cross my legs, and standing for more than fifteen minutes was painful. Often, I found myself out of breath at the slightest exertion—I hated bending over. Even if I was just laughing, I couldn't catch a breath.

I was 32 years old and I felt like an old fat lady.

One evening, we were taking photos of our family in the living room. Just before the shutter snapped, I pushed the kids out in front of me. In that moment, I realized that I would never be able to accept myself at this size. I hated how I looked, and now I was hiding behind my children.

I knew I had to do something, and I had a pretty good idea of what. I didn't go all out on a crash diet or anything like that. I just made a decision that I was going to do what I needed to do to be a happier, healthier person. For me, that meant eating healthy food in acceptable portion sizes and exercising regularly.

It's been a long journey—three years and counting—but it's been worth every minute. The other day, I went to the mall with my teen daughters and tried on some jeans at Old Navy. "Oh, my gosh, Mom, you look so good!" one of my girls said.

"I do, don't I? Where's your dad?" I joked, pretty pleased with my reflection in the mirror.

More than being happy with how I look, though, I'm a different kind of mother to my kids. Now, I'm the one to say, "Hey, let's go for a walk." When I'm out walking with them, we have some one-on-one time to talk that we never had when I was just sitting around the house. We recently went to Disney World for five days—I wouldn't have lasted even five hours before!

I am so grateful to have a loving and open relationship with my children. Our home is a safe place where we can all build up each other's confidence. I feel good about myself, stronger than I ever was, and happy about my "new" motherhood. I'm not the fat mom anymore and, with God's help, I'm never going to be her again.

Leah Gonzalez and her husband, Freddy, live in Jacksonville, North Carolina, with their three children, Elizabeth, Itzel, and Alex. Leah blogs about her weight loss journey at My New Ending (www.leahs-new-ending. blogspot.com). "A New Mom" is based on the blog post "Mom's Weird" (July 2, 2012) and adapted with the author's permission.

14

MY MOM PURSE

MEGAN FERREE COBB

CHICAGO, ILLINOIS

Back before I had kids, I chose purses based on their color. Their style. The feel of the leather. The way they smelled. Their ability to add that perfect *je ne sais quoi* to an outfit.

But now that I'm a mom, I select a handbag based on how big a truck I can drive into it without grazing a side-view mirror or smashing up the grill. Gone are the days of the dainty, leopard-skin clutch with lipstick-red leather trim and a tiny gold-beaded clasp. No, these days, what I really need is a three-car garage with padded shoulder straps.

Case in point: After a weekend of running around all over town with the family, playing, shopping, eating out, and going to a minor league baseball game, I noticed mysterious groaning noises coming from my generously-proportioned, bright orange hobo bag. On closer inspection, I discovered the bag was being stretched and pulled to its very breaking point by the sheer volume of familial necessities I'd managed to cram inside it over the course of two days. I had everything I needed in that gaping maw, you can be sure.

The only trouble with having everything you could ever possibly need crammed into your bag—plus a little more—is that when you really do need something, there's no way you'll ever actually find it. My daughter slipped down a hill at the baseball game, scraping her knee, and I spent the next three and a half innings rummaging around for a bandage I knew was in there, somewhere. I never found it.

So, on Monday morning, I hauled Purse-zilla up onto the countertop and unloaded it. Ha! I've come a long way since the days of wallet-keys-lipstick-and-out-the-door. My mom purse could eat that cute leopard print clutch for lunch and still have room for an umbrella, a baby blanket, and a Mini Cooper.

Here's what spilled out of my mom purse onto the counter:

- a wallet and a set of keys
- a blue figure-eight teething ring
- a small pair of pink sunglasses
- lipstick, lip gloss, a pot of lip balm, a tube of lip sunscreen, and a ChapStick
- four pink wooden daisy beads, three lavender wooden heart beads, and one wooden faerie bead (That necklace from the faerie birthday party two months ago must have broken.)
- an empty Tic-Tac box
- a pen from a mutual fund company
- a bottle of orange ginger hand lotion and a travel-sized baby lotion
- an emery board
- seven quarters

- a tiny measuring tape/keychain combo (price tag still affixed)
- a Pampered Chef catalog
- a one-gallon zippy bag containing a dozen baby wipes
- a one-quart zippy bag containing a handful of crushed goldfish crackers
- a one-gallon zippy bag containing nothing
- my iPhone and a camera
- another lipstick
- brown sunglasses
- two dental-appointment cards (from last year)
- a blue plastic spoon
- a hair elastic
- three, ahem, "girl things"
- a receipt for two muffins, a cookie, and two coffees dated July 1, 2009
- a baseball parking pass and three baseball ticket stubs
- a tin of breath mints (four left)
- more orange ginger lotion
- hand sanitizer
- a couple of size 4 pull-ups and a pair of Dora underpants
- a half-full sippy cup
- a half-full water bottle
- a cup of Cheerios
- a tub of unsweetened applesauce
- five individually wrapped wet wipes from the barbecue joint
- my Transformer fold-up hairbrush
- a second set of keys (just in case)
- a sun hat decorated with blue sharks

- half a green crayon
- three Matchbox cars
- a tiny screwdriver for repairing eyeglasses, and
- a handful of assorted crumbs, fuzz-balls, and other uniden-
tifiable bits of debris

Hidden in a small side pocket, I finally located the three missing
SpongeBob bandages, an alcohol swab, and a bottle of children's acet-
aminophen, along with a half-eaten mini candy cane that had been
licked into a very sharp point. (Ouch!)

Sometimes, the treasure-laden mom purse serves as more than just
a mobile child-care and emergency-everything kit, doing double duty
as a constant source of entertainment for my children. My 3-year-
old son has a particular affinity for spelunking around in its bowels
when I'm not paying attention and creatively using its contents to
wreak havoc.

Not too long ago, he managed to climb up onto the dryer (where
the mom purse sleeps at night), extract the car remote, engage the
door-lock and alarm buttons, and then carefully drop the remote into
the black abyss behind the dryer.

With the car alarm blaring not ten feet from my head, I rushed to
disconnect the dryer from the vent, drag it three feet into the laundry
room, vault up and over the dryer, and retrieve the remote—all the
while my ears pounding and both children wailing about the noise, at
which point I discovered that after its plunge to the floor, the remote
no longer worked.

I retreated to the kitchen counter and, above the racket, attempted
to shout soothing words over my shoulder to the kids as I painstak-
ingly dismantled the remote using the eyeglass screwdriver (from my

purse, of course) so I could jiggle its battery back into place. Having accomplished that, I screwed the whole thing back together and hastily pressed the buttons to deactivate the alarm and unlock the doors.

I breathed a sigh of relief and turned around to find my son, clad in his adorable monkey jammies, smiling cheerfully back at me, the big hobo bag drooping heavily off one shoulder. In his little fist, he was gripping a tube of lipstick, and his face was covered from ear to ear in opalescent pink scrawls.

Unlike me, my son can always find exactly what he's looking for in my mom purse.

Megan Ferree Cobb is a native Southerner who currently lives in the Chicago area with her husband and two kids. When she's not rifling around in her mom purse, she's serving up laughter and inspiration at her blog, Fried Okra (www.friedokra4me.blogspot.com). A storyteller to her core, Megan's blog is a mix of thoughts on marriage, parenting, style, food—and whatever else pops into her mind. "My Mom Purse" originally appeared in Megan's blog as "What's in Your Mom Purse?" (August 31, 2009) and was adapted by her for this book.

15

THE MEAN MOM

LYNN COWELL

CHARLOTTE, NORTH CAROLINA

Standing in line for a concert on a hot day in the Blue Ridge Mountains, our family of five—me, my husband, our son, and our two teen daughters—had plenty of time for people watching.

As girls and guys made their way to the back of the line, I took it upon myself to point out all the immodest clothing on display.

"Why on earth would she wear a skirt that short in public!"

"Those pants are way too low!"

"I can't believe she feels comfortable with her bra showing like that!"

As though on parade, the girls in skimpy clothing passed us by. I just couldn't seem to hold back from voicing my opinion on each girl and her style choices.

I must have shared quite a few of these insightful comments, because my oldest daughter finally spoke up.

"Mom, you are being mean!" she said, exasperated.

Mean? *Who, me?* I was shocked. I wasn't being mean. Not at all! *I'm simply taking advantage of a teaching moment with my girls*, I thought, defending myself. *I'm just pointing out to them how immodest these girls are.*

I pretty much thought I knew mean when I saw it. As a child, I was a mean girl myself, at least for a while, before I matured and realized that Christians shouldn't act that way. I remember one time in the fourth grade, there was a boy in my class whose pants were so big he had to bunch them together at the waist with a belt to keep them up. My girlfriends and I giggled about it and called him "bubble butt."

As soon as my own girls started school, we had to deal with mean. By the third grade, my oldest daughter was 5-foot-6 and was singled out for her height. One day, she got off the bus and ran into the house, holding herself together until she was safely inside. But once inside the door, she burst into tears of grief. The kids on the bus had called her an awful name, one that had hurt her deeply.

Even teachers weren't immune from making my daughter feel bad. One day, I planned a special surprise for my daughter, and I came in to have lunch with her. When her class entered the cafeteria, I saw the line of children enter in ascending order of height. First the girls, then the boys, and then . . . my precious daughter. The teacher had always lined up her students from shortest to tallest. It never crossed her mind that she was singling out my daughter and making her feel self-conscious and out of place.

My younger daughter suffers from the other extreme. Now in high school, she's just 5-foot-2. She gets jibes about the other end of the spectrum. "Are you done growing already or what?" kids have teased her.

Throughout their lives, my daughters have lived under the microscope of public and peer scrutiny. "You talk too much," some said, while others complained, "You keep too much to yourself."

"You dress like a grandma," taunted some of the kids. "Why was your bra strap showing on your Facebook picture?" countered others.

When you're a teen, you just can't seem to win, no matter what you do. If you're bright, you'll be shunned for knowing all the answers. If you're less than a top student, you'll be called dumb, or worse.

From their peers to outspoken parents, my daughters have had to hold up under the barrage of other people's opinions. They haven't liked it, and as their mother, neither have I.

So, when my daughter accused me of being mean, I resisted the accusation. I was simply standing on the side of right, wasn't I?

Wrong! While I tried to tell myself I was simply pointing out to my daughters how not to dress, in the end I had to admit my daughter was right. I was putting myself in the position of judge and jury. I wasn't teaching my girls how not to dress. My girls already knew and modeled modesty—I'd been teaching them that since they were five years old.

Instead, I was just being mean—a mean mom. By my thoughtless words and actions, I was teaching my kids how to judge other people. I was teaching them to be mean girls. When I pointed out others' flaws, I modeled for my kids a judgmental heart. A heart so crowded with unkind thoughts that there is no room for the grace that I receive from my Savior freely every single day of my life.

As women, we may not even realize we're being mean, especially when it involves each other. One time, my husband and I were standing in the lobby during the intermission of a choir concert. After a few minutes, my husband said to me, "How come whenever a woman comes into a room, all the other women size her up?" I protested that it wasn't true. But when I thought about it, I had to admit he was right. I recalled all the times I'd looked at another woman and harbored harsh thoughts about her hair or her outfit or her makeup, whatever it was that didn't meet my exacting standards.

After my daughter pointed out that I was being mean, my children and I made a pact with each other: You point out to me when I'm being mean, and I'll do the same for you. Whether it's gossiping about other people or putting another person down, we call each other on it. It's a risky thing to invite your child's commentary on your words and actions. At first, having my child point out when I was making an unkind remark was uncomfortable. I grew up in an era when parents were always right, no matter what. I never would have said anything about personal failings to my parents!

But by allowing this openness in our family, we are helping each other learn to demonstrate compassion and grace, and not only demonstrate it, but truly feel it in our hearts. Because we've made this a family issue, rather than just me correcting my kids, we've all been brought to a deeper level of kindness. Since that night at the concert, I've learned that mean girls come from mean mamas—but they don't have to.

Lynn Cowell and her husband, Greg, live in Charlotte, North Carolina, with their three children. She is a speaker with Proverbs 31 Ministries, for whom she writes an online devotional feature, "Encouragement for Today." She writes for many magazines, including Susie Mag *and Focus on the Family's* Thriving Family *(www.thrivingfamily.com). She is the author of several books, including* His Revolutionary Love *(Standard, 2011), and her most recent book,* Devotions for a Revolutionary Year *(Standard, 2012). Lynn blogs at her website, www.LynnCowell.com.*

16

AND HOPE REMAINS

JOANN CANTRELL

CRANBERRY TOWNSHIP, PENNSYLVANIA

"Hope" is the thing with feathers—
That perches in the soul—
And sings the tune without the words—
And never stops—at all—

EMILY DICKINSON

I was like a mother to my brother, Don, who was ten years younger than me. He was born with a deformed heart, and the doctors said he wouldn't live past the age of five. They didn't give us much hope.

But my brother defied the odds. He had surgery twice, once when he was 10 years old and again when he was 18, but he grew into adulthood, attended college, married, and had three children. Through it all, we dared to hope that Don would claim victory over his defective heart.

One day at work, though, Don began to feel unwell. He drove himself home, where he collapsed and went into cardiac arrest. A medevac helicopter transported him to the hospital. It's an image that is forever seared into my mind—the helicopter carrying my brother as it lands on the hospital roof that cold and rainy January night.

At the hospital, they shocked Don's heart seven times and administered CPR for 15 minutes before they got a heartbeat. Given the passage of time, his brain was likely to be severely damaged, and the neurologist prepared us for the worst. She seemed intent on keeping us from irrational hope. When I said that we'd pray for a miracle, she said noncommittally, "You can if you want to."

Though he was alive, Don remained unresponsive. Doctors began talking to us about the tough decisions that we might face in the days to come, decisions that would determine whether Don would live or die. Yet, we were used to nurturing hope in the most dire of situations—Don had always rallied before. And, miraculously, two days later, Don woke up.

For fifty days, from January to March, we stayed by Don's side, praying for a miracle. It's hard to maintain hope in a hospital room day after day. One night, while I was sleeping in a chair next to Don's bedside in the critical care unit, I was awakened suddenly when a hospital worker came into the room. Seeing that I was startled, he squeezed my hand in reassurance and said, "Have hope."

Don's heart was so damaged that he was put on a waiting list for a heart transplant. Doctors reckoned that he was strong enough to undergo the procedure, and indeed, in March he was released from the hospital. Just ten days after he came home, much sooner than any of us expected, the call came in that a heart was available. We were overjoyed! Our hope was being rewarded!

The surgery went well. Our spirits were buoyed. Yet just two days after the operation, Don passed away. He was only 36 years old. I was at his bedside when he took his last breath. Without fully realizing it, we had spent our final hours with our beloved Don—son, brother, husband, father. Our grief crushed us. For months, I couldn't stop crying.

Though I was like a mother to Don, I was privileged to have my own son. Soon after Don went into the hospital in January, my son Matthew and his wife Kathy broke the news to us that they were expecting a baby. In our time of sorrow, this news became a ray of hope for us.

The day Kathy went into labor, she and Matthew surprised me by asking me to be in the delivery room with them. And, so, in the same year that Don died, I was honored to witness the miracle of birth. Where once I stood at the bedside of my dying brother, I now stood beside my son and daughter-in-law as their baby came into the world. A baby girl.

As he cradled his newborn daughter, Matthew looked up at me, and he said simply, "Hope. Her name is going to be Hope."

My grief over Don's loss had been so hard to come to terms with. Yet, now, I was bathed in the joy of the circle of life. Having lost all hope, I gained it once again through the miracle of a baby girl—my first granddaughter.

Joann Cantrell is a freelance writer, editor, and storyteller who lives in Cranberry Township, Pennsylvania. She writes frequently for the Pittsburgh Post-Gazette. *On December 25, 2006, the* Post-Gazette *featured her first-person story about her brother's death, "The Year of Finding Hope," for which she later won a Golden Quill Award from The Press Club of Western Pennsylvania. "And Hope Remains" is a retelling of her experience.*

17

THE FORBIDDEN RIDE

HEIDI BYLSMA

COOL, CALIFORNIA

Giddy and apprehensive, my two children and I stood waiting next to the pasture gate at a friend's ranch. We'd traveled to the ranch in a neighboring state to meet our new horse Dodger for the first time.

My friend was sure that this 15-year-old mustang would be perfect for our family. When my 10-year-old son Daniel heard that our new horse was a mustang, he made his intentions clear—the new horse *had* to belong to *him*.

Because he is autistic, many things in Daniel's life have presented challenges. What others take for granted, Daniel struggles to achieve or, in frustration, simply abandons. His daily battles with the world have been heartbreaking for me as his mother.

Just as I had found fulfillment in riding horses, so I thought Daniel might blossom on the back of a horse. But, during one of his first riding lessons, a horse ran away with Daniel at a full gallop and he was hurled into the pipe corral fencing at the arena. He suffered little physical injury, but the injuries to his confidence were devastating. From that moment on, he lost all interest in riding.

Yet, now, something about the possibility of having a mustang as his own pony rekindled a spark, a seemingly dead ember, in Daniel's heart. So, here we were, ready to take a chance on a horse that we had never even seen.

Dodger stood rigid in the pasture, tense, wide eyed. My friend said Dodger would not allow a human to approach and halter him without the benefit of a grain bucket. The carrots we had so eagerly brought with us would be wasted, as Dodger wouldn't take food from a human hand.

Surely this horse can't be right for our family! I thought. How could a horse with "issues" possibly mesh with a boy like our Daniel? I knew that Dodger had come through a program for wild mustangs brought in from federally managed lands, but I wasn't prepared for this emotionally fragile animal that would shrink from our very presence. Physically, he had scars and indentations on his face that spoke of rough handling in his past, but obviously it was his spirit that was far more damaged.

While the adults droned on, becoming tired of waiting, Daniel silently slipped out to the pasture, halter in hand, to introduce himself to his new friend. Triumphantly, he led Dodger over to meet us. Later that day, we were astonished when Dodger relished a carrot Daniel offered to him.

Dodger came home with us a month later. As we worked with him, Dodger would occasionally tremble, seemingly convinced we were going to beat him, or even kill him. We noticed that he often drew inside of himself, or, as our trainer would say, he would "go to that safe place in his mind."

Only one person could approach Dodger without causing this emotional shutdown—Daniel. Content merely to brush his pony or to care for his hoofs, Daniel spent hours with Dodger down in the pasture. Sometimes, Dodger followed Daniel around the forested hillside pasture, seeming to thrive in the comfort and camaraderie he garnered from the presence of his special boy.

Incredibly, an unlikely bridge seemed to be forming, one that linked the world of an abused mustang pony with that of a socially challenged 10-year-old boy. But, still, Daniel showed little interest in riding.

A few months later, though, Daniel announced that he would like to ride Dodger. I was thrilled! So, on a mild June morning, we headed down the hill to the pasture. Dodger's shrill whinny greeted us. Poking over the gate to welcome us in a wet nuzzle, Dodger stood at the gate, eager to give the gift of himself.

Helmeted and ready to ride, my son haltered Dodger and pre- pared to ride him bareback. But suddenly, I realized that I had left his clip-on rein back at the trailer. I had to go back for it before Daniel could ride.

"I'll only be gone for a few minutes," I told Daniel. The rule in our family is never to mount a horse without an adult present, and Daniel knew that.

I retrieved the rein, and started back down to the corral.

Descending the hill, rein in hand, I was shocked to see Daniel astride Dodger. Daniel hadn't waited for me to return! He had climbed onto the feeding trough—our makeshift mounting block—and Dodger had apparently "sided up" and invited Daniel to join him for a ride.

I stopped to watch horse and rider. Daniel had only a lead rope attached to Dodger's halter, but they were negotiating serpentines, figure eights, and circles like pros. Daniel was grinning from ear to ear as the two of them promenaded around the corral.

In my heart, I wanted to be angry with Daniel for breaking such a vital safety rule. But as I watched the two partners, the lightness and softness with which Dodger responded to Daniel's unschooled cues took my breath away. For about ten minutes, they rode with grace and precision.

My son may have violated an immutable rule, but I just couldn't rebuke him. Everything had come together in one breathtaking instant: Daniel's newfound confidence and the invitation of this reticent pony. It was a moment that was meant to be. Together, Dodger and Daniel had found their safe place with each other.

Because of Dodger, my son has been forever changed. He has been infused with a confidence bestowed by the kind of special relationship that we horse lovers can sometimes only dream about. In his willingness to become the solicitous partner to a young autistic boy, Dodger has carried all of us so far.

Heidi Bylsma and her family moved to the country to fulfill her life-long dream of having horses in her backyard. She homeschooled their children, Daniel and Michaela, who are both in college. She collaborated on the book Thin Within *by Judy Halliday RN, and Arthur Halliday, MD (Thomas Nelson, 2005), and provided editorial support for the book* Raising Fit Kids in a Fat World *by Judy Halliday, RN, and Joani Jack, MD (Regal, 2008). Visit Heidi on the web at www.heidibylsma.com. "The Forbidden Ride" was originally published as "A Bridge Beyond" in* Chicken Soup for the Horse Lover's Soul, *volume 2 (HCI, 2006) and adapted with permission.*

18

MOTHER'S DAY MANIA

LORI GARD

MILL RIVER, PRINCE EDWARD ISLAND

Wearily, I eye the clock next to the bed. It's not even 6 A.M. and I've been jostled awake by a snoring husband and a pillow-thieving 5-year-old. Happy Mother's Day!

I crawl out of bed to ready myself for this day of festivities. It's Sunday, so all six of us need to get dressed and out the door for church. Not only that, but it's my daughter Maggie's tenth birthday as well. That means the traditional bedside birthday video, present opening, and a special birthday breakfast.

Sandwiched between all of this will be phone calls to my mother, my sisters, and my sisters-in-law to wish them a happy Mother's Day, as well as phone calls from both sets of grandparents wishing Maggie a happy birthday. Later in the day, the family will gather at a restaurant for lunch. Later still, I'll head over to the school where I teach kindergarten to prepare lesson plans for tomorrow, and then it's back to church for the evening service.

Whew! The sun isn't even up yet and the day stretches out before me like a rubber band, ready to snap under the slightest pressure.

The day starts with my tradition of waking the birthday child with the birthday song and catching her first moments on video. It's a moment I usually cherish, but today my 11-year-old son, Sam, is indignant because he hears me and thinks we've left him out of the present opening. Angry and accusatory words pour out of his mouth. I try my best to soothe him and explain that the gifts have not, in fact, been opened, and he hasn't missed a thing. Already, I'm cast into the role of peacemaker and the sun is just coming up over the horizon.

After smoothing things out, mom, dad, and the happy troops head downstairs to open gifts with the birthday girl. As soon as Maggie finishes opening her presents, MaryAnne, our 5-year-old, co-opts the most alluring of the gifts—a Zuca figure-skating bag. It's turquoise, it has lots of zippers, and the wheels light up. MaryAnne decides it's the perfect suitcase to cart her stuffed animals around in. With awe, the rest of us watch her ability to so easily get her own way with her sister. Man-i-pu-la-tor. We will see more where this came from before night-fall brings this day to a close, mark my words.

To appease each child, I schedule in time slots with the bag, and again, a full-bore blow-out is avoided. We'll save that glorious event for breakfast.

While I am in the shower, my husband slips out to Tim Hortons to pick up a special Mother's Day breakfast—three breakfast sand-wiches, two coffees, and a box of Timbits. Only three of us like egg on a biscuit, so you'd think that three sandwiches would be enough to go around. But you'd be wrong. The three inoffensive sandwiches unaccountably become the center of an all-out brawl. While some are vying for the sandwiches, others are fighting to stave off the interlop-ers. Again, playing peacemaker, I divide my sandwich. Sam is angry that his mother, who is supposedly being honored today, is being cheated out of her sandwich, and he leaves the table in a huff. Those who remain get a stern talking to. Meanwhile, the half sandwich goes uneaten.

In a minor miracle, after breakfast we manage to get ready for church in record time and arrive before 10 A.M. Sunday school has begun—the first time we've managed this feat all year. This in itself is a Mother's Day gift to cherish. But I can't rest just yet—I'm the church pianist, and at the 11 A.M. service, not only do I play the piano, I also sing a solo that I've prepared.

After church, it's off to the restaurant for lunch. It's a Chinese restaurant and about the only game in town, so the place is packed. We're the last members of my husband's family to arrive, so hubby and I are relegated to the far end of the table amid the ten grandchildren, separated by acres of table from the other grown-ups. We can see adults, and we can hear adult conversation off in the distance, but we cannot join in. I stare at a picture on the wall while I eat my Mother's Day lunch in silence.

At some point, nature calls and I head off to the restroom. As I near completion of my visit to the ladies room, I lean over to grab some toilet paper from the dispenser, and the whole rig comes off the wall and crashes down on my head. Dazed, I secure the unit, and try again. Once more, the dispenser dislodges and lands on my head. In a neat bit of acrobatics, I prop it up with my aching head and manage to secure the paper needed, all the while nervously checking under the stall for any recognizable shoes on the other side. Lucky for me, my exploits have gone unnoticed.

I wrap things up and get out of there in record time. If anything, this Mother's Day has been all about setting new personal bests in the area of speediness. For that, I can give myself a big pat on the back.

Returning to the table, and still quarantined from the grown-ups, I reflect on Mother's Days past. Ten years earlier, Mother's Day had also found us at a restaurant. At the time, my husband and I had just one child, Sam, and he was a toddler. I was pregnant and close to my due date, so he wasn't going to be an only child for much longer. In the restaurant, we worked hard to keep him busy at the table, and I remember thinking what a lot of work it was. One child! *If only I had known!*

Later that same night, after I tucked my sweet Sam into bed, I took a picture of him asleep surrounded by all his books, and I wondered to myself about a mother's love. I remember thinking: *Will I be able to love another child as much as I love Sam?* I wanted to hold this precious moment in my heart for all time.

Before long, I learned the answer to that question. At 1 A.M. I went into labor, and by 8:30 that morning I had become a mother for the second time, this time to our daughter Maggie. Before I even saw her or held her, I was in love with her. She was a part of me, just as Sam was a part of me. A mother's heart makes room.

Now, being a mother of four, I've been the recipient of many, many Mother's Day cards and wishes from my children down through the years. I keep them all—they're dear to my heart. But, to be honest, the one whose words come immediately to mind is a card I received from Maggie a few years ago. After wishing me a happy Mother's Day, she closed with this touching sentiment: "P.S. By the way, I want an iPod Touch. It's only $99.99."

So as this Mother's Day nears a close, I don't know about all you other moms out there, but it is somewhat of a relief for me. The day carries so many expectations and so much pressure. I'm not sure I can handle more than one day of special treatment per year—it might just do me in. But whether I like it or not, next Sunday is coming, and it's bound to be a doozy. It's my birthday, and I can only imagine what insanity will ensue.

Lori Gard lives in Mill River, Prince Edward Island, with her husband, Brian, and their four children, Samuel, Maggie, Sarah, and MaryAnne. Lori is a kindergarten teacher and a writer who blogs at Pursuit of a Joyful Life (http://pursuitofajoyfullife.wordpress.com). She contributes "Dispatches from Down East" for the Huffington Post, *and her work has also appeared on the Power of Moms website. She is active in her community and church and heads up the breakfast program at her school. "Mother's Day Mania" first appeared as "Mother's Day Joy" on Pursuit of a Joyful Life (May 14, 2012) and is adapted with permission.*

19

MILESTONES

MY INDEPENDENT CHILD

NAOMI CASSATA
CALLAHAN, FLORIDA

When Holly, my firstborn, came into the world, I wasn't so sure she was really from my gene pool. You'll never meet a more independent child. I'm surprised she wasn't born on Independence Day just to prove a point. In fact, when it came time to cut the umbilical cord, I'm pretty sure she handed my husband the scissors.

I don't think I even knew the true meaning of independence until Holly came along. Before she was born, I thought little girls were supposed to be dependent, shy, and clingy. At least that described me as a child. I was shy and hesitant, especially in new situations. I have a younger sister, but unlike many girls who don't want their baby sisters tagging along after them, I was glad for her company. It was a comfort to have her around so I didn't have to face things on my own.

I remember so clearly my first day of school. The night before, I was excited about going to kindergarten. I busied myself choosing which outfit I was going to wear, pestering my mom to promise me she would drop me off in the morning. Yet, when I was faced with the reality of being alone—of being away from my mom—I couldn't handle it. My mother lingered in the classroom to get me settled in, but settling in was not on my to-do list that day. When it came time to say goodbye, I bawled, I screamed, I clung to her as she tried to make her way to the door. I desperately wanted her to take me with her! The teacher held me and comforted me as I watched my mother disappear from my sight.

Holly's first day of preschool was a complete contrast. She faced the day with an abundance of confidence. A little too much confidence, if you ask me. Not even 4 years old yet, she was as ready as she could be, pigtails bobbing and Tinker Bell backpack in place. She was eager to explore new terrain outside the safe confines of our home, even though it didn't include me or her baby brother. Before I even had a chance to sign her in at school, she had walked past me and her teacher to explore her new surroundings. If I didn't know better, I'd say she was a preschool pro. As all the other kids hugged and kissed their parents goodbye, my little Holly didn't look back—she didn't even wave.

It wasn't very long before one day, as I pulled into the preschool parking lot, she informed me that I didn't have to sign her in that day. "I'll sign myself in, and you can stay in the car," she announced. Seriously, whose child is she, really?!

If I'm honest with myself, I have to admit my feelings were a little hurt that Holly could so easily detach herself from me. I envied all the other mothers whose children gave them hugs and kisses when they said their goodbyes. But I knew that Holly was enjoying herself at school, so I tried not to dwell on my own feelings.

Still, cutting the apron strings is not an easy thing to do. Change that involves our children is not always welcome. Even when it is a good change, it can be hard to accept, and I hear it only gets more difficult. "Wait until they're teenagers," parents of older children have warned me. *Let me just get past preschool*, I'm thinking.

Even before that first day of school, Holly had showed her independent streak. When our son was born a few years ago, she stayed with my husband's parents for a few days. At one point I called to talk with her, but she was having such a good time at Grandma and Grandpa's that she refused to come to the phone!

I've come to realize it isn't my daughter's independence that really troubles me, but rather my own fears that are my biggest obstacle. Letting go and trusting God to take good care of my children, even when I'm not present, is the only way to suppress my worries. I have to trust that God can do a much better job at protecting my children than I ever can.

Holly will get bigger, smarter, and even more independent as the years go by. As much as I want to keep her forever under the safety of my wing, I realize it's only through letting her try her wings a little at a time that she will learn to fly on her own. Already, she's gone to the beach with friends and to the county fair with her grandparents— oceans and crowds are just two of the many things that make me nervous about my children's safety!

I'm proud of my daughter's boldness. Even so, I can't help but be secretly pleased that these days she isn't always wielding her scissors around my apron strings. My parents live just seven minutes away, and one night Holly was having an overnight with them. But at 10 o'clock that night, we got a call—our little independent child missed her mommy and daddy and wanted to come home. And that was more than fine with me.

Naomi Cassata lives in Callahan, Florida, with her husband, James, and their three children, Holly, Christian, and Caleb, and they are expecting their fourth child. Naomi is a writer who contributes articles to Focus on the Family's Thriving Family *magazine (www.thrivingfamily.com).*

THE $20,000 BREAKFAST
STEPHANIE STAPLES
WINNIPEG, MANITOBA

There is no way to be a perfect mother,
and a million ways to be a good one.
JILL CHURCHILL

It's been called "The $20,000 Breakfast."

We scrimped and saved and tweaked our budget to come up with the $5,000 a year we needed to send our son to St. Paul's, a four-year Jesuit-run high school. The years went by in a flash, and now we mothers of graduating sons were being treated to a morning of celebration on the Friday before Mother's Day.

Although this annual celebration of the graduating class was quite hush-hush, we had heard whispers about it from other moms who had experienced it. Still, we had only a small idea of what to expect.

So, there we were, we moms, all seated next to our grown sons—150 young men of 17 and 18 years old—crammed into a hot, crowded auditorium on a muggy May morning.

The day began with a celebration service. Each boy pinned a rose on his mother's collar and volunteer moms from other graduating classes handed out tissue packets. *Tissues? How strange*, I thought to myself.

Yet over the next three hours, the need for tissues became more than apparent.

In turn, each boy—big strapping football players, small late bloomers, smart kids, challenging kids, quiet kids—was given one minute with the microphone. One minute to bare his soul in front of 300 others. One minute to look into his mother's eyes and tell her what was in his heart.

Most of the boys were anxious, nervous, and more than a little petrified. We moms could feel their anxiety and it was rubbing off on us as we waited for the ceremony to begin.

With sweaty palms and quivering voice, the first boy began. Then, one by one, each boy stood up with his mom, introduced her by name, and began.

Some boys had been up all night searching for the perfect words, some had been working on his speech for months. Many boys started with, "This is my beautiful Mom," and that was enough to start our waterworks flowing.

This is what the boys said.

"I didn't really want to go to this school when all my friends were going to a 'regular' school, but I am so glad you made me come here. I will send my own son here, too."

"Thank you, Mom, for the thousands of miles you've driven, for always giving up the best piece of chicken and the biggest slice of cake for me."

"Thank you for the years and years of packed lunches, Mom."

"Thank you, Mom, for *not* packing my lunch, for believing me capable of doing it on my own." (My son!)

"I'm sorry for the late nights and the missed curfews, Mom."

"I'm sorry for not being respectful sometimes and for leaving my bedroom and the bathroom a shambles."

"Mom, I have worked for months on this speech and I can't stop crying long enough to read it to you."

"Mom, you mean the world to me. I love you."

Some boys dug out wrinkled papers from their suit pockets, some just spoke from the heart. Some sang songs written especially for the day, some read poems, and some recited quotes. Some boys cried and could barely utter a word. Some crooned songs their mothers had sung to them as a child. One young man started to sing "You are my sunshine," but couldn't get through it. Still, he wouldn't let go of the microphone or his mom until he choked out every last word.

Each boy's speech was unique and beautiful, poignant and sincere. Each one perfect. Never have I heard the word "mommy" used by so many grown boys, unapologetic, unabashed, uninhibited. Some draped themselves over their mom's shoulders as they choked out the words that had been buried for so long—"I love you's" that had never been said and hugs that had never been shared.

Each boy was raw, honest, and genuine, and at their words, we moms felt our hearts skip a beat, or stop beating altogether, before feeling it again, louder and more powerful than ever before.

For three hours, we were privy to 150 of the most intimate moments a mother and son could possibly share. How could it be that each moment seemed frozen in time, yet went by in such a blur?

We moms spoke no words that morning. Mouthing "I love you" was about the most we could manage. Besides, this was not our day to speak; it was our day to listen. Just listen.

Soon, we realized that it was not just what our sons were saying to *us* that was important. These boys were speaking to mothers everywhere, on behalf of boys everywhere. They were speaking for the boys who could not find the words or the courage or the right time or the right place. They were speaking for the boy who wanted to say "I'm sorry," who wanted to forgive, who wanted to start fresh, who wanted to tell his mom that she was his rock, his mentor, his guide. It was a thank you given for things that can never, ever be repaid by boys who understood that to be God's truth.

I began the day thinking that the ceremony was all about validating me as a mom of a grown son. To my surprise and delight, it was so much more. It was a day to validate all mothers and the unique position of motherhood. It was a joy and a privilege to be in that room, and when it was over, moms and sons alike were emotionally spent.

Many of us moms—or perhaps all of us—wonder whether we are doing enough, being enough, giving enough to our sons. We question whether anything we say gets through, whether our sons know what they mean to us, whether they get it. My questions were unequivocally answered on that beautiful day in May, when the 150 "one minutes" were over and we all gathered in the schoolyard to pray aloud and plant a tree in honor of the journey we had all taken together.

The $20,000 Breakfast. In my book, it was a bargain.

Stephanie Staples is a motivational speaker in Winnipeg, Manitoba, whose business, Your Life Unlimited (www.YourLifeUnlimited.ca), focuses on people working in healthcare settings. She has published a book, When Enlightening Strikes: Creating a Mindset for Uncommon Success *(BookBaby, 2011), which is a book of personal growth strategies for leading a happier life.*

20

KEEPING MY MOTHERHOOD BADGE

HELEN L. HOOVER
LINDALE, TEXAS

Let us not become weary in doing good,
for at the proper time we will reap a harvest if we do not give up.

GALATIANS 6:9

Why in the world did I ever want to be a mother? I fumed. *Those kids are ungrateful, selfish brats! I should have finished college. I should have been a nurse. I should never have had children!* The patio swing creaked as I conducted my pity party. Sunlight filtered through the summer clouds, but my world was dark.

My husband, Larry, had supported my decision to be a stay-at-home mother. I wanted to raise our three children myself so I would have time to teach them a godly lifestyle. *My* kids wouldn't come home from school to an empty house! I looked forward to greeting them at the door and hearing about their day. Their friendships would need my supervision. I envisioned homework and science projects as rewarding family times. I loved to sew and would enjoy making their costumes for school activities. Decorating cookies with them would be so much fun!

My expectations for motherhood were high—until reality hit me full force that day. I don't remember exactly what the kids did to incite my despair. At ages 6, 13, and 16, they all rebelled at times, of course, but normally not all three of them in one day.

But, idealistically, I had always thought our offspring would appreciate the many sacrifices I was making for their well-being. That they would be grateful even. Not so! They just wanted more stuff, fancy gadgets, and name brand clothing. My money-saving meals were met with disdain. They grudgingly did yard work and cleaned their rooms. They wanted to run free all day without parental supervision.

Larry arrived home from work later that day, expecting that I would greet him at the door, as usual, and have supper started. Instead, searching the house for me, he found the kids alone watching television and playing with toys.

"Where's your mother?"

"Don't know."

Finally, Larry headed outside and found me swaying on the swing, head down, burdened by the uncooperative behavior of our kids. Quietly, he stood before me, waiting for me to begin.

"I'm giving up my motherhood badge."

"Why would you want to do that?" he asked, gently.

"I'm through being a mother! I'm tired of coping with their behavior," I complained. "They pout, complain, and refuse to help me. There's no sense in me trying to be a good mother. It's a thankless job."

"Well, if you're quitting, so am I," Larry responded.

"*What?* Why?" I replied, puzzled.

I couldn't see why he would want to quit. *He* wasn't the one dealing with them on a 24-hour basis. I had no pity for him—after all, he got time off while he was at work.

"Because you are not leaving me with those ungrateful monsters all by myself!" he said.

A smile came to my face then, and I began to see the humor in the situation.

"Come on, we can do this together," Larry coaxed me. "They're probably sorry by now for causing you problems." He pulled me up into his arms for a tender hug. "I love you," he said, sweetly.

Pushing back from me and looking into my eyes, he said, "What's for supper? I'll help you."

Larry's compassion broke the crisis—his loving support encouraged me to resume my motherhood responsibilities that day.

In the weeks and months that followed, I began to notice the unrealistic expectations I had placed on my children. Young minds couldn't recognize when I needed help. Expecting them to be enthusiastic about every meal I prepared didn't allow for their preferences. It was beyond their understanding to appreciate my concern for their well-being around strangers. My desire for them to always behave in a godly manner didn't allow for spiritual growth. I became aware that changes were needed in my life as well as in theirs.

It is probably just as well that I don't remember what my children did that day to upset me so. God doesn't remember my sins either.

Over the years, my children have more than redeemed themselves. They make my day with bear hugs, give me sweet cards of thanks, and attend to me with kind, caring comments. They include Larry and me in special times with their friends. They have helped us through tough times and given us thoughtful gifts. When our oldest son left for college, he told us, "You two have been wonderful parents. Thank you." At the open house for our new home, our younger son presented me with a couch throw in my favorite colors, and our daughter planned a surprise fiftieth birthday party for me.

I'm glad I didn't give up on motherhood that day. Despite the stressful moments of motherhood, I realize now that I would not have wanted to miss a single moment of my children's growing-up years. I would have forfeited so many blessings as they matured into delightful and responsible adults. Today, I am honored to wear my motherhood badge with pride.

Helen L. Hoover lives in Lindale, Texas, and enjoys sewing, knitting, and traveling. She and her husband volunteer with the Sower Ministry for retired Christian RV'ers. Their four grandchildren and three great-grandchildren give them great joy. Helen has had stories published in three anthologies, Chicken Soup for the Soul, Love is a Verb, *and* Deliver Me. *She has had devotionals and personal stories published with Evangel, Word Aflame, Standard,* LIVE, *WordAction Publishing, the* Quiet Hour, *Light and Life Communications, Victory in Grace,* Lutheran Digest, *and* The Secret Place.

21

A Voice in the Dark

A N N E T T E   G E R O Y

K E R R V I L L E ,   T E X A S

"Get up and go to Ginny's!"

A resounding voice jolted me awake in the cold, dark morning hours. I had been tossing all night long on the lumpy dorm-room bed at the summer aquatic camp where I was to be a counselor. I had not slept well and was not ready to leave my warm blanket behind. Not yet.

The voice sounded again with commanding authority, bouncing off the bare gray walls. "Get up and go to Ginny's!"

"What was *that*?" I wondered, my puzzled mind swirling with questions. Yet, my eyelids began closing again.

Suddenly, I bolted upright, my heart pounding.

"Lord, is that you?" I asked.

"Get up and go—now!"

"Okay, okay," I answered. "I hear you!"

Quickly, I scanned the stark, tomb-like room for my clothes and a hair brush. The icy tiled floor beneath my feet sent me scurrying

for the bathroom. Disoriented, I screeched to a halt. Where was
the bathroom?

I had just arrived at camp the day before, and I had not fully
unpacked. I scrambled to stuff a few loose items into my suitcase,
while I worried over a believable excuse to give the camp director for
leaving. I felt certain that telling him the Lord woke me up and told
me to go to my daughter's would brand me as certifiably crazy.

Understandably, the director was disgruntled as I mumbled a
few words of apology for leaving him in the lurch. I rushed across
the college campus, determined but still asking myself, *Have you lost
your mind?*

My daughter, Ginny, had a 2-year-old daughter and a three-month
old son. To her great chagrin, she was pregnant again. She had
called the previous Friday to tell me the news. She was concerned
because she had experienced a couple of fainting spells that she could
not explain.

She fainted for the first time in the grocery store. She became light
headed and slumped suddenly to the concrete floor. Her children
were in the grocery cart, unattended, while she lay in a heap. Help
came quickly, but she was confused and embarrassed, and afraid of
being out of control while she was with her children. A day later she
almost fainted again while getting out of her car.

Ginny had never fainted before in her life, so of course she thought
it might have something to do with the pregnancy. I agreed and suggested she talk with her doctor right away. When she called her doctor's office to discuss her concerns, a nurse assured her the fainting
spells could be the result of a hormonal imbalance caused by becoming pregnant again so quickly.

"Call back if the problem continues," she said briskly, putting an end to the conversation. Her abruptness seemed to imply that Ginny was overly excitable and wasting the nurse's precious time.

After driving for an hour in the predawn, I arrived at Ginny's apartment and knocked on the door. It was just 7 A.M.

"Ann, what are you doing here?" my son-in-law, Robert, asked when he opened the door, shocked to see me standing there.

"I'm here to take care of the children while you take Ginny to the doctor," I said firmly. And then I whispered, "All I know is the Lord woke me up and told me to come. So I came."

Ginny padded into the living room looking rumpled and pale. Confused, she echoed her husband's question. As I repeated my story, I began to feel very foolish. Had I just imagined the voice?

Ginny's response, typical for her, was no nonsense.

"If the Lord told you to come so I could go to the doctor, then I guess I'd better go," she said.

They gave me instructions on where to find bottles, formula, and diapers, and then they rushed off to the doctor's office without even making an appointment. I waited anxiously as I soothed my hungry and confused granddaughter, sterilized bottle parts, and paced with the baby. Doubts assailed me again as I circled the apartment. Was there really a serious issue or had I disrupted their routine for nothing? I almost felt embarrassed, but not quite.

Several hours later, Robert called to say that Ginny had been admitted to the hospital. She had passed out again on the way to the doctor's office. After examining her, the doctor determined that Ginny was bleeding internally from an ectopic pregnancy. The days-old embryo had attached to her fallopian tube, producing a lesion similar to an ulcer. The internal bleeding had caused a severe drop in her blood pressure, resulting in the fainting spells.

Ginny's condition was so precarious that the doctor would not even allow them to drive across the parking lot to the hospital. She called an ambulance to deliver her a few hundred yards to the emergency room.

"The emergency room doctors said Ginny might have died if they hadn't seen her when they did," Robert told me. "They were amazed at how lucky she was to have reported to the office that morning."

Relieved and thankful, I silently acknowledged the true source of our "luck."

Following surgery and a night in the hospital to monitor her blood pressure, Ginny was sent home for some bed rest. The clothes I had packed with camp in mind were perfect for taking care of two small children—children who still had a mother because I listened when the Lord said, "Get up and go to Ginny's!"

Annette Geroy is a lay minister with Mount Horeb House Ministries in Kerrville, Texas, where she works extensively with women who have suffered sexual abuse. She tells the story of her own healing journey in Looking with New Eyes, My Journey from Bondage to Freedom *(Guardian Books, 2006). The ministry's home on the web is www.mounthorebministries.com.*

22

IN THE COMPANY OF HEROES

DAWN LILLY

NEWCASTLE, WASHINGTON

No mother with two toddlers in tow expects to slip into a room undetected, but I certainly hadn't counted on drawing the attention of every single service member in the waiting area of the Kadena Air Base dental office. One airman slapped my older son a high-five as we walked by and a sergeant gave him a thumb's up.

"Cool T-shirt," he said. "I like Superman, too."

Four-year-old Jason beamed as the superhero's logo stretched taut against his tiny chest of steel.

"Me too!" chimed in his brother.

Two-year-old Adam struck a pose in the middle of the crowded room and thrust his arm up in the air.

"Masters of the Universe!" he yelled, waving a muscled action figure dressed in a Speedo and wielding a sword and shield.

"That's not Superman!" Jason said with disgust. "That's He-Man!"

Laughter erupted and a few soldiers even clapped, transforming the usually staid waiting room into a Monday morning comedy club.

Flushed with embarrassment, I grabbed both boys and led them to a row of open seats.

"Sit still and be quiet," I whispered, digging into my backpack and pulling out crayons and coloring books. "I'm going to check in with the receptionist, and I don't want either of you to move or say a word. Understood?"

Jason and Adam bobbed their heads and looked at me with wide-eyed innocence.

"Cute boys, Ma'am," the receptionist said when I finally reached his counter, what seemed like days later.

"I hope you still feel that way when we finally get called in to see the dentist," I answered, only half joking.

He smiled and handed back our ID cards. Returning to my seat, I stepped through a minefield of spit-polished boots and thanked my boys for their exemplary behavior.

"Look what I did!" Jason slapped his picture down on my lap and handed me his crayon.

Coloring time was obviously over, and as I scrambled to find something else to occupy my boys, a camouflaged soldier handed me an office copy of *Highlights* magazine.

"My daughter likes the hidden pictures," he said.

"Thanks," I said, grateful that he understood my plight and relieved to buy a few more moments of peace and quiet.

One by one the servicemen were called back to see the dentist. I scratched backs, rubbed feet and shoulders, played Tic-Tac-Toe, anything to keep my boys quiet. Adam laid his head on my lap, and I brushed my fingers through his hair. He was nearly asleep when Jason leaned over and tugged on my arm.

"Mommy, will you suck on my ear?" he said, loud and clear. My hand clenched.

"Ouch!" Adam cried. I released my grip on his hair, rubbed his head, and apologized. I turned to speak to Jason just as he decided I hadn't heard him the first time.

"Mommy," Jason shouted, "Will you . . ."

"Shhhhh!"

He jerked back and wiped my spit off his face. Surprise and confusion crossed his face.

"Not now," I hissed between clenched teeth. "Later. When . . . We . . . Get . . . Home. Okay?"

I enunciated each and every syllable. Slowly. Then I stabbed him with The Look. Both boys stared at me like I had just ripped the heads off their He-Man figures.

Someone cleared his throat, and I looked up. My head pounded as the blood rushed to my face. All eyes locked on me, and I slumped in my chair, wishing fervently to melt into it, to escape the stares and scrutiny.

I was no pervert! Surely these men had mamas who kissed the crook of their neck and nibbled on their ears when they were little? And speaking of mamas, where were all our female soldiers? Why was I the only woman in a room full of men? How had I managed to pick a day and time when no other woman had scheduled an appointment?

"Mrs. Lilly," the receptionist called from the front of the room.

I sucked the last breath out of the room, and exhaled what I thought was a silent prayer. "Thank you, God!"

Someone chuckled, and my head shot up. *Did I say that out loud?* Heat rushed to my cheeks as winks and smiles greeted me. My heart lifted and relief flooded me. There were either a good number of affectionate fathers in that room, or many of these men had mamas who had loved on them when they were little, too.

I grabbed our things and ushered the boys to the front of the room. They marched forward and I followed—an arsenal of toys in hand and my head held high—the lone mama in the company of heroes.

Dawn Lilly and her husband, Dave, live in Newcastle, Washington. She and her hero raised their two boys while Dave served in the Air Force. Her sons have grown, married, and blessed her with six grandchildren she loves to kiss (and nibble on). She has written for numerous publications, including Guideposts, Seek, Evangel, *and* Chicken Soup for the Soul. *She has written for DaySpring cards and is currently working on her first novel. Visit her home on the web at www.dawnmlilly.com.*

23

THE GOOD LIFE

STEPHANIE WARD

PLANO, TEXAS

"I want Stephanie to take my kids," the young woman said at her custody hearing.

With those words, my life was turned upside down.

I had spent most of my adult life avoiding motherhood, and I was pretty successful at it. I owned an art gallery in Dallas and represented artists of national renown. I had worked as a journalist, and I owned rental properties. I sat on nonprofit boards and traveled extensively. I dated great guys, owned a lovely home, drove a Mercedes, and threw lavish parties.

It was a good life. A good, good life.

Yet something was missing, it seemed to me. I wanted to give back to my community in some way, so I started hunting around for volunteer work. One day, I was looking through the newspaper when I saw an ad from an organization looking for people to provide homes for battered women.

I answered the ad, and thirty days later I took in an 18-year-old girl and her baby daughter. Clarissa was white, and the baby a mixed race, and because of that her parents had thrown her out of the house the day she came home from the hospital. She spent her first night alone with her baby sleeping under a playground slide. She had been living on the street for some time.

We had a rocky time of it. Clarissa was streetwise in the way homeless people have to be, and I laid down the law. I made her go to church with me, forced her to jog with me, and took her to work with me at the art gallery. She didn't like it one bit. It wasn't long before she left my house.

Fourteen years passed, and we had no contact. But she began to enter my mind almost daily, and eventually I heard a voice inside my head saying, *Call her!* But I didn't even remember her name. And then one day when I was sitting in my office, I got a phone call. It was Clarissa.

"Stephanie," she said. "You may not remember me. I lived with you fourteen years ago."

After saying that, she questioned me rapidly me about my life, my marital status, and whether I had any children. Then she said, "I've had three other children since I lived with you, and my youngest two are wards of the state."

Clarissa had been arrested a few times and spent some time in jail since she had lived with me. She had been diagnosed with lupus and doctors had seen a suspicious spot on her brain. While she was hospitalized, the children's father took them to a babysitter, but when no one came for the children after two days, the babysitter called the police. They came and took the children away.

"My kids are in foster care right now," she finished. Hearing this, I was a little apprehensive about her motive for calling.

"Are you calling me to help you get your kids back?" I asked her.

"No," she answered. "My mommy days are over."

"Are you calling me to *take* your kids?" I asked. Clarissa chuckled at my response.

"You don't ask just *anybody* to take your children," she said. "But I remember the things that you taught me, the way that you lived, and I trust you."

After two months of phone calls back and forth, I offered to give Clarissa a ride to her custody hearing. At the hearing, Clarissa's attorney reprimanded her.

"You've had a year to get your act together and to comply with the requirements for gaining back your children. Yet, you've done nothing to show that you want your kids back," she said.

On hearing this, Clarissa—this tough, hardened street girl—began to cry. Seeing her so broken, I started crying, too.

Although we asked whether it would be possible for Clarissa to reclaim her children after some agreed upon time, her attorney said there was no chance of that.

Defeated, Clarissa gave in.

"I don't want my children to be like me, Stephanie," she said between sobs. "I want them to be like you."

Six weeks later, a white station wagon pulled up in front of my house and the children were handed over to me. Crissah was 3 years old when she came to me, and her brother Casey was just 18 months old.

Me? I was 46 years old.

Once I opened my door to the children, the life I had once known vanished. The demands of motherhood forced me to close my art gallery, lose my rental properties, and fall into poverty. My friends drifted away. Even my church family didn't know how to help me. I struggled with depression as I mourned the self I had once been. The thought of suicide entered my head more than once. It was several years before I got into counseling, regained my footing, started a new business, and was able to support my family better.

Today, my kids and I are doing well. They're A students, they're happy-go-lucky, and they have such positive spirits. They're good, decent people and they make me laugh. On tough days, my son can sense my mood and will come to me for a cuddle on the couch. I have found such joy in motherhood. There's something so healing about the love between a mother and her children.

Still, you might be tempted to ask, "Why on earth did she do it?" I sure asked myself that question plenty of times. The bottom line is this: I didn't want to say no to God. To me, it was clear that he brought Clarissa and her children into my life for just this reason. As I walked out of that custody hearing, the children's guardian said to me, "I hope God blesses you." And he surely has.

Stephanie Ward lives in Plano, Texas, with her children and is the owner of Red Lime Media (http://redlimemedia.net), a social media marketing business that caters to small and midsize businesses. Stephanie credits her adjustment to motherhood in part to a volunteer project she started when she realized that single mothers rarely get gifts for Christmas. Since 2008, Gifts for Moms has provided hundreds of Christmas gifts for struggling single moms with the help of generous donors and volunteers.

24

A BABYWEARER'S CONFESSIONS

HYACYNTH WORTH

LAKE COUNTY, ILLINOIS

Dear Mr. Graco Swing,

I love you like the crazy my kids drive me.

Today, you—you with your weird little animal pattern—have made having two children easier than I ever imagined. You must have some secret kind of charm, with your constant motion and your rickety-crickety motor sounds, because little baby EJ has been out like a light several times today for more than ten minutes at a time.

You see, baby EJ really, *really* likes to be moving at all times. And even as a babywearing mama committed to holding my babies close, I just can't keep moving 24/7. So, you've allowed me to do many things today—including, but not limited to:

- shower for the first time in, oh, maybe three or four days,
- fix a dinner that required more than pulling something out of the freezer and pressing buttons on the microwave,
- make it to the bathroom in time, without having to keep the baby nestling in my arms in a constant jiggle while I simultaneously got into position,

- read that stupid *Mr. Brown Can Moo! Can You?* book at least seventeen times in a row to a very happy Dr. Seuss-loving older brother.

Normally, you see, I have to walk around the house with the baby strapped to me in a carrier or nestled in my arms, happily cooing away, in order to accomplish my daily tasks. This works out fine—or, more accurately—it works out fine as long as I never stop moving. *Never,* as in not for one single moment.

And that's where you've got me—and the hundreds of dollars worth of baby carriers I've bought over the years—beat. The truth is that at some point, the mommy simply runs out of steam and needs a break from lugging around the 12-pound infant. And, given the laws of physics, carriers only move as much as the person they are tied to.

You, Mr. Graco Swing, never cease to move. You are a moving machine, literally. And baby EJ loves that about you.

I know, Mr. Graco Swing, that when my first baby was born, I carelessly tossed you aside for those baby carriers, like a frat boy drops his empty beer can on the ground when he finds there's a keg at the party. For that, I sincerely apologize. Those lonely years in the basement must have been chilly and dreary for you.

But, truthfully, my first baby preferred those expensive, fancyschmancy carriers. I'm happy for you now, because this baby seems to really enjoy the cheap plastic animals that are stuck to your cheap plastic tray, not to mention your ability to never tire of your continuous movement.

But I just want you to know that if I had batteries, I could do that, too.

So, you win for now. But I'll tell you this—I'm keeping my stash of baby carriers, because you can't really replace me. You can't take the baby to cool places like the park or the zoo like I can, can you? But, during the day, you can take him to the land of sleep and dreams. And for now, I'll take it.

Sincerely,
A very tired babywearing mommy

——— ——

Dear fellow babywearers,

Please don't vote to demote me from my leadership role in the Lake County babywearing group simply because I was loving on the swing today. I'm tired. I cannot move all day long. I promise to wrap baby EJ two times per day for the rest of the month to make up for my swing affinity. I swear, this whole swing thing—it means nothing to me! *Nothing!* Please don't hold an intervention and confiscate all of my carriers and redistribute them to more dedicated babywearers. I swear—this is a one-time thing. It'll never happen again. Really.

Sincerely,
Your very tired, swing-loving, babywearing co-leader

Hyacynth Worth lives in Lake County, Illinois, with her husband and two children. She is a writer who contributes to CBS Chicago's "Best of Family" section and blogs at Undercover Mother (www.undercovermother.net). She is co-founder of the Bigger Picture Blogs (www.biggerpictureblogs. wordpress.com) and is at work on an e-book titled The Vine Life. *"A Babywearer's Confessions" appeared as "Letters of Intent: Dear Mr. Grace Swing" on Undercover Mother (October 23, 2009) and is reprinted and adapted with permission.*

25

DUMPSTER-DIVING MAMA

SARAH COYNE

JOPLIN, MISSOURI

There is no friendship, no love,
like that of a mother for her child.
HENRY WARD BEECHER

The summer season at my daughter Mia's preschool is shortened to
two mornings a week for six weeks. It isn't her favorite place to be.

The classroom is different, most of the kids are different, and to top
it off she's one of only two girls in her class. The other girl's name is also
Mia, and I think sharing a name with a new friend is making her feel odd.
She isn't the most adaptable little girl, and change upsets her equilibrium
so much that she's been clinging to me, crying, and refusing to leave me.

But by the end of her time at preschool—her time of painting and
running and sprinklering and laughing—she's her happy self again.
My big 4-year-old, ready to be independent and bossy once more.

A few days ago, as I collected her and her belongings after a water
play day at school, I watched her skip happily down the hallway to the

front doors. Her ponytail was swinging over her back, marking time with each leap and skip of her legs, and she was completely happy. I was, too. My baby, Lauren, was in my arms and my shoulders were loaded down with Mia's swimsuit, towel, water shoes, book bag, and lunchbox. Everything was good. We all climbed into the car, buckling in and settling down for a snack on the drive home.

Suddenly, Mia burst into tears. Hers weren't shy, quiet tears, but loud, fit-preceding tears of terror. Dramatic tears, which are, in fact, her forte.

"Your *flowers*," she wailed, starting to kick against her car seat. "We forgot your *flowers!*"

I had no idea what she was talking about. The teacher had said nothing about flowers, and Mia's wailing words were working their way toward incoherence.

Eventually, I understood that she had left flowers—flowers of some sort—in her classroom, on the countertop, by the sink. And they were for me. Especially for me, and we couldn't leave without them, because she'd worked so hard on them.

I was torn.

Both girls were already strapped into their seats, and the midday sun was turning our car into a sauna. The classroom was at the far end of the building, and naptime was due to start any minute. Home was where we needed to be, but my sweet girl—my sweet little girl who was having trouble transitioning into a new setting—needed something else, something more.

Deciding on a plan, I started the car and drove right up to the front doors of the school. I got the attention of the front desk secretary, and she agreed to watch the girls in the car while I ran to the other end of the school.

When I reached Mia's classroom, I was out of breath from running, and I croaked out what little I could to Mia's teacher. *"Mia's flowers?"* I gasped.

"Oh, yes, I'm sorry," she apologized. "I already threw those away out in the hall. I didn't think she'd be back for them."

Hearing the teacher's words, I was crushed for Mia's sake and, honestly, already dreading the tears I knew she'd resurrect when I didn't return with her precious flowers.

"But they're probably easy enough to reach," the teacher added, heading out into the hallway toward the trashcan.

She took the lid off, and there, mixed among papers and lunch wrappers and heaven knows what else, were dozens of tiny, white, clover flowers. *Dozens.* Scattered over and under everything. Mia's entire morning's work—flowers for her mama.

I leaned over the garbage can for a few minutes, picking out as many of the flowers as I could see, avoiding the soggy, smelly food bits and dirty napkins. It was hardly glamorous work, but it felt important. It felt like I was affirming that I'd clearly seen and heard my daughter's attempt to show me her love.

As I walked back to the car, the crumpled bunch of weedy flowers clutched in my fist, I thought about how long it must have taken her to pick all of those flowers. I thought about the other kids running and screaming and playing around her, while she squatted alone, searching for beautiful additions to her bouquet.

I thought about the smile on her face when she gives me any flower from any ditch or any field. She's so thoughtful and caring that sometimes it melts me.

It melts me right into a garbage-digging fool.

When I returned to the car, Mia's face was mottled red and tear-streaked, but she gasped and smiled when she saw the flowers.

"But where are the rest of them?" she asked. I had salvaged maybe only a third of what I'd seen in the garbage can.

"Some of them got lost," I said, "but these flowers in my hand are the *best* ones."

I kissed Mia on her head and clutched the flowers, thanking my daughter for her thoughtful gift—for thinking of me and knowing how much I'd appreciate the bouquet.

Even though I had to rummage through the trash bin to find it.

At home, I covered the stems in water, letting the flowers regain some of their perk and stature. Their beauty and worth had already been redeemed, though, in the eyes of one little girl and her sappy, dumpster-diving mama.

Sarah Coyne lives in Joplin, Missouri, with her husband, Justin, and their three children, Mia, Lauren, and Landon. Sarah writes a weekly parenting column for the Joplin Globe, *and she hopes to write more as her kids grow. "My dream is to be a work-at-home author," she says, "Or maybe to own a bakery and a used book store, combining two of the things I love best in the world: books and pastries!" "Dumpster-diving Mama" originally appeared as "The Flower Girl & The Garbage Picker" on her blog, This Heavenly Life, www.thisheavenlylife.blogspot.com (July 1, 2010), and is reprinted and adapted with permission.*

26

DREAMS FROM MY MOTHER

TERRY GRAHL

DETROIT, MICHIGAN

Nothing happens unless first a dream.

CARL SANDBURG

A polka-dotted pillow changed my life.

I'm not talking about a pretty, decorative pillow trimmed in a wide feminine ruffle. No—I'm talking about a bare pillow lying on the stained mattress of a prison bed.

I am a wife and the mother of four children. I enjoy a safe, stable life in my home in Michigan. My husband has a good job, and my four kids are all wonderful young people. Up until six years ago, I had a successful interior decorating business. I would come into people's homes and "heal" their rooms.

One day I took a phone call from a gentleman asking for help. He was the event coordinator of a shelter for homeless people in Pontiac and was looking for volunteers to spruce up the shelter.

"We would be so grateful, even if you just came in and painted one wall," he said.

To be honest, my first reaction was fear. I was afraid. I had never been to a shelter. I didn't know what I'd see. But I decided to visit before I made any decision.

On the day of my visit, the director showed me around. The shelter was huge—it housed more than a hundred men and seventy women and children. In addition to housing, it offered programs to help people get back on their feet.

The place was depressing. Peeling paint and cracked, unfinished drywall. Metal doors and moldy, sagging ceilings. Broken steps. The chapel was encased in gloomy, brown paneling. The women's dorm was furnished with metal prison bunk beds and lockers that had broken doors. The carpet was stained and worn. I took photos as I went from room to room.

I was overwhelmed as I thought about what needed to be done. I was leaning toward a gentle refusal of help. At most, I thought I might offer to work on the chapel.

But I had a lingering feeling of despair, having seen the living conditions of these women and their children. I didn't live like that. Why should they have to? Finally, I decided to look through the photos before calling the shelter.

That's when I saw the pillow. It was lying on the stained and sagging mattress of a metal bunk bed that was pushed against an unfinished sheet rock wall. It didn't even have a pillowcase. It was just a bare pillow with a pattern on its cover—a pattern of big, white polka dots.

I have always loved polka dots. I've worn them and I've decorated with them. They're cheerful and they lift your spirits. It's a safe pattern that has no sharp edges.

When I saw that pillow, I heard a voice speak to me. *Trust me,*
it said.

Now, I've never been one to hear voices, so I knew this was a word
from God. From that very moment, I knew I would be prepared to do
whatever I could to bring hope to these women and children. I wanted
to help them realize their worth—to help them dream.

I've always been a big dreamer. My teachers and classmates used
to tease me. "Snap out of it, Terry!" they'd say. My mother instilled
this in me and my four siblings. She was a creative woman. She made
all our clothes and cooked all our meals from scratch. We were poor,
so poor that we had to move twelve times, and sometimes all we had
were food stamps for groceries. But my mom always made us feel
secure and happy. For my mother, making a home where her children
felt safe and where our spirits could soar was as important as keeping
us fed and clothed.

My mother passed her imagination on to me. When my children
were young, they'd ask me to tell them bedtime stories. Not stories
from books, but stories of my own. I'd start off, "We're in front of
our house, and you're on your bike. You're flying! Flying through the
sky. . . ." My stories were all about dreams.

But living my secure, stable adult life, I'd given up on my dreams.
Going into clients' homes, I didn't feel my dreams soaring. I felt them
contracting. I never heard God's voice in a client's home. But I heard it
at the shelter.

I closed down my decorating business and founded a nonprofit to
transform the lives of people living in shelters. The Pontiac shelter
was my first project. Donors and volunteers joined me in turning
the shelter into a welcoming space in which women and children
can blossom.

And it's not just paint on the walls. The women's own creativity is sparked by workshops and projects that allow their talents to emerge—baking and sewing, painting murals, crocheting. They begin to soar.

"I am *not* what that room used to make me feel like—unworthy, depressed, and scared," one woman told me, emotion catching in her voice. "I feel that I am worthy now."

It wasn't an easy road to take. I struggled at first to find donors and volunteers. Our family missed the income my job provided. But every time I felt low, God sent me a special word to keep me going. One day, in a parking lot, I was in my car crying after yet another rejection from a store I had hoped to sign on as a donor. A man I didn't know came up to me and said, "God is with you. Don't give up!" How could I ignore that?

There is such power in a mother's love! My mother's love for me gave me the courage to dream big. Women in shelters all around the country are dreaming and fulfilling their dreams for themselves and their children. My own children are being shaped by the vision. They know, as I do, that if you are blessed you need to share that blessing, to put footsteps to your prayers. All you have to do is listen to that voice inside of you.

Terry Grahl is the visionary chief executive officer of Enchanted Makeovers, which she founded to support women and children who are rebuilding their lives by transforming their environments into places that inspire behavioral and psychological change. She and her husband, Scott, live in Detroit with their four children, David, Kevin, Todd, and Tracey. Visit the Enchanted Makeovers website at www.enchantedmakeovers.org.

27

ECHOES OF MERCY

SHARON BETTERS

BEAR, DELAWARE

Angels descending, bring from above
Echoes of mercy, whispers of love.

FANNY J. CROSBY

It used to haunt me: *Why did we let him drive that night?* But I've had to accept that the accident wasn't our fault. We had no way of knowing.

Our family had spent a quiet evening at home. All four of our young adult children were at home with us. I was happy to be surrounded by my children. Our youngest son, 16-year-old Mark, and his brother, Dan, practiced some songs they were preparing for a youth concert at our church—Mark on the drums, Dan on the guitar. Later in the evening, Mark watched television with Kelly, a friend from school whose father had dropped her off at our house for the first time.

After their program ended at 10 o'clock, Mark asked if he could drive Kelly home. Mark had just recently gotten his license, but we felt that he had proven himself a good driver. It wasn't raining, and the night was clear, so we thought it was safe to say yes.

At about 10:15, I said my goodbyes to Kelly as my husband saw Mark and his friend to the door. Chuck told Mark to be careful, reminded him that he could use the car phone if necessary, and finished by saying that he loved him. "I love you, too, Dad," Mark responded.

Chuck and I started to get ready for bed, although we planned to stay up until Mark was safely home. About 45 minutes later, we were startled to hear the phone ring. I answered it, expecting to hear Mark's voice.

"Mrs. Betters?" a woman began. "I'm calling from the Christiana Hospital. Your son Mark has been in an accident."

"Is he okay?" I asked, fear rising in my throat.

The caller hesitated.

"He's in critical condition," she answered. "You need to come right away."

Chuck and I hurried to get dressed and out the door, shouting to our other children as we went. In the car, we sped to the hospital, willing drivers to get out of our way, lights to turn green. Driving down a four-lane divided highway, we came on an accident scene. It was the same road Mark would have taken to get to Kelly's house.

On the other side of the highway, we saw a mangled car. In the dark, we couldn't make out what kind of car it was. But I knew. As the lights of the emergency vehicles flashed, I peered into the darkness and spotted a yellow blanket hanging out of the car's trunk. One of our beach blankets.

At the hospital, a nurse met us at the door of the emergency room. She led us down a hallway and turned toward a room on the left. My husband is a pastor; he knew about that room. It was the room the hospital reserved for notifying families of a death. "Is our son dead?" he asked the nurse. The nurse nodded. Yes.

I heard screaming—a strangled, smothered voice screaming, "No! No! No!" I didn't know that it was my voice. I collapsed against my husband, beating on his chest, my body limp as he tried to move with me into the room. We soon learned that Kelly had also died in the accident.

That night—July 6, 1993—was the beginning of a long road of wrestling with God. I could not believe that the God I professed to love had so cruelly taken my beloved child from me. We never even learned for sure what happened that night. I couldn't believe that I would never see Mark's smile again, never hear his voice again, never hug him again. Day after day, I sobbed until late at night, and the next morning, I would wake up sobbing again. I didn't think that I could go on. I ached for Mark with a mother's deep longing.

The days, weeks, and months following Mark's death crept by in an agony of hopelessness. I struggled to cope within our devastated family. The words of Jesus, suffering on the cross, filled my ears: "My God, my God, why have you forsaken me?" I pleaded with God to heal me. Even though I knew he was present, had always known he was present, he didn't take away my grief. He didn't give me what my heart wanted most—my child back. *How could I ever trust him again?*

The following spring, to honor Mark's birthday, which falls on May 11, I planted a rose bush in my back garden. I chose a white rose that, to me, symbolized the peace and purity of God that I longed to experience in the aftermath of Mark's death.

The bush rarely bloomed that first year and I was sure that it had died. But the next spring, just as I started to pull it out of the ground, I noticed a few green leaves on the stems, so I left it alone.

That summer, I kept an eye on the bush. I didn't expect to see anything, really, and I didn't even prune the bush, but I fervently hoped that it hadn't died. I was still barely coping with Mark's absence. I didn't think I could handle one more reminder of his death.

One day, while in the back yard, I looked at the bush and gasped. My struggling bush bore two lovely, long-stemmed white roses! I knew immediately why they were there—one for Mark and one for Kelly. And, sure enough, when those two roses died, two more appeared. All that summer, every day, two perfect white roses graced that rose bush—no more, no less.

Before Mark's death, I was skeptical when people said they received signs from above after the loss of a loved one. I thought they might be creating a connection where there was only coincidence. But from the depth of my own grief, God's gift of these roses taught me that the veil between this world and the next is gossamer thin.

God sends echoes of mercy to the broken-hearted, love letters to the bereaved. Just as lovers have a private language that no one else can understand, God speaks intimately to the hearts of those who mourn. These signs, these treasures in darkness, have been specially designed by him to allow us to trust him with our grief.

Sharon Betters lives in Bear, Delaware, with her husband, Charles, senior pastor of Glasgow Presbyterian Reformed Church. They are the parents of four children, their youngest one in heaven, and grandparents to fourteen grandchildren. After Mark's death, the couple founded MARKInc Ministries (www.markinc.org) to produce and distribute free resources for grieving people. Sharon is a retreat and women's event speaker and the author of several books, including Treasures in Darkness: A Grieving

Mother Shares Her Heart *(P&R, 2005)*, Treasures of Faith: Living Boldly in View of God's Promises *(P&R, 1999), and* Treasures of Encouragement: Women Helping Women in the Church *(P&R, 1996).*

"Echoes of Mercy" is adapted from Sharon's blog post, "Echoes of Mercy, Love Letters from God" (July 6, 2010), with the author's permission.

28

A Sure Sign

ERICA KOSAL

RALEIGH, NORTH CAROLINA

My husband, Jim, was in his late 40s when he started to experience some odd symptoms. At first, it was just headaches and neck pain. He thought maybe he had the flu, something that was going around at work.

But the symptoms didn't lift, and it got to the point where he was always tired and sleeping a lot. I began to wonder if he was suffering from depression.

More worrisome, Jim realized he was having trouble with daily tasks, like twisting off bottle caps, and when he held out his arms, he could see his skin sort of popping, as if there were a snake under his skin.

Jim didn't want to alarm me, so he tried to keep his symptoms hidden. But he started searching the internet trying to figure out what was wrong. One night, I walked into his office, where he was sitting at his computer, staring at the screen. "I think I need to see a neurologist," he said.

The thought didn't alarm me. Jim had always been healthy, and it didn't even enter my mind that he might be seriously ill.

So, Jim saw a neurologist, and after some tests the doctor said Jim might have a syndrome that was affecting his nervous system, but that it wasn't likely a cause for major concern. "Your test results are not normal, but they're not abnormal," the doctor said. "You could come back in six months, and everything might be perfectly normal."

We were relieved to hear those words, but even so, the doctor suggested that we consult another neurologist at Duke University Hospital for a second opinion.

When we met with the neurologist at Duke, he rattled off a list of five possible diagnoses, including HIV, renal cancer, and amyotrophic lateral sclerosis (ALS), or Lou Gehrig's disease. Jim underwent a battery of tests to rule out the possibilities. Oddly, I found myself praying it would be renal cancer. It seemed the least terrifying diagnosis.

When we met with the doctor a second time, he greeted us with a smile.

"I have good news for you. We know what you're suffering from," he said. "It's ALS."

We were stunned. *What? ALS? Did he really say that was good news?* I couldn't even look at Jim. He was staring straight ahead. A social worker jumped right in and started rattling on about the progress of the fatal disease and the difficulties we would face. I just sat there, tears streaming down my face.

We were numb for a long time. Jim wanted to learn as much as he could about slowing down the progress of the disease. For my part, my mind was whirling. *Should we move closer to my mom? Should we buy a ranch house? What will my life be like without my husband? What will it be like for my son to not have a father?*

We had a son, and I had had a lot of difficulty getting pregnant with him. I underwent fertility testing and three years of medical intervention before we were successful. Braxton was now a year old and just learning how to walk. My heart ached for him.

To lift his spirits, Jim decided to go on a ski trip with some of his friends. While he was gone, I began to feel sick myself.

One night, Jim called from the ski lodge. He was tired and depressed. The trip wasn't going well at all. His legs were weak, and he had to go to bed early while his friends stayed up and had fun together. But I had good news for him.

"Jim, things look bad now, but I know that everything is going to be okay," I told him, excited and confident. "Trust me, I know."

Jim was puzzled. "What? What do you mean?" he asked.

"I'm pregnant!" I announced triumphantly.

After I began to feel unwell, I had taken a pregnancy test. I truly never thought it was possible for me to get pregnant, yet the test was unmistakably positive. There was no doubt about it!

I took the fact that I was able to get pregnant as a sign. I knew in my heart that this was no coincidence. I felt that I was carrying a baby who was sent to us to let us know that we were going to be okay.

All along, I had doubted Jim's diagnosis of ALS—I just had a gut feeling that something wasn't right. We devoured books and movies about people with Jim's symptoms. We kept after his doctors to consider other possibilities.

It wasn't long before we got our miracle. After further testing, Jim's symptoms turned out to be Lyme disease. *Not ALS!* This time the news really *was* good. His doctors started him on a course of intravenous antibiotics.

About this time, we began to think about names for our baby—a girl, we discovered—and we were going back and forth between two names. Eventually, we settled on Annalise.

One day, I got a phone call from my mother.

"Do you know what the name Annalise means?" she asked, her voice full of excitement. "Gift from God!"

How appropriate! We couldn't have chosen a better name for our little girl. She was definitely our miracle baby, and surely a gift from God when we needed hope the most.

Erica Kosal and her husband, Jim Young, live in Raleigh, North Carolina, with their two children, Braxton and Annalise. She teaches biology at North Carolina Wesleyan College and together with her husband has founded Bounce to Resilience (www.bouncetoresilience.com) to coach, counsel, and speak about bouncing back from hardships, setbacks, and adversity. Erica has written about her family's struggle in Miracles for Daddy: A Family's Inspirational Fight against a Modern Medical Goliath, *which released from Burro Publishing in December 2012.*

NOTE: Jim's battle for health continues, yet they've seen some improvement in the past few months. Annalise continues to lift their spirits. "No one can bring a smile to Jim's face faster than daddy's little girl," Erica says.

29

BATTER UP

NANCY B. KENNEDY

HOPEWELL, NEW JERSEY

Little League baseball is a very good thing
because it keeps the parents off the streets.

YOGI BERRA

I never imagined myself as a baseball mom. Despite a brief infatuation with the Mets during their 1986 championship season, I pretty much remained true to my book-loving, opera-going, foodie-fanatic self.

But then I had a son.

Early on, it was evident that Evan would draw me back into the game. I saw that grass-green, diamond-shaped gleam in his eye one day when he was still a toddler.

That day, we were watching a movie about a kids' baseball team whose hopes are riding on their bruiser of a slugger to win the championship game for them against their archrivals.

"It's a beautiful day for baseball!" the announcer declares as parents and grandparents pour in, filling the stands.

The game begins, and the matchup is a good one. The lead goes back and forth between the two teams. By the bottom of the ninth, the visiting team is ahead by one, and the home team is up. Two kids get on base, two kids go down, and the hometown boys are down to their final out. But all is well—it's the top of the order and their slugger is up. The day is saved!

The pitcher digs in. He hurls the ball over the plate, a big fat strike. But the batter, Casey-like, shrugs it off. "That ain't my style," the narrator intones. "Steee-riiiike one!" the umpire calls. The at-bat continues, the tension mounts, until finally the count is full. One final offering sails over the plate and . . . the batter swings and misses.

As the ball thunks into the catcher's glove, the camera pans in slow motion around the field and across the dugout. One by one, the faces of the players and coaches fall in dismay, eyes wide and mouths gaping. I glanced over to see how Evan was taking the heartbreaking strikeout, but instead of tears, I saw a spark in his eye.

Something about that scene struck Evan's fancy. He had us replay the strikeout over and over—both on the screen and in person. In his play room, he would mime swinging the bat, and then my husband and I—strategically placed around the room—would approximate shock and disbelief as best we could, although it's difficult to manage when you're trying hard not to laugh.

As Evan got older and began to play with blocks, he would build elaborate baseball stadiums, complete with ticket booths, gates, seating, lights, scoreboards, and concession stands. He laid down dust cloths for the infield and scouted players from among the ranks of his action figures, Playmobil characters, and Lego guys. Pirates, superheroes, medieval knights, and race car drivers sat cheek-to-jowl on the dugout benches. The game would begin; the ball would fly out of the park, and Evan would scoot his players around the bases.

All would be well, the game progressing nicely, the score 101 (Evan) to nothing (me), until our Border Collie would wander out onto the field wagging her bushy tail and wreaking canine havoc in the stadium. "Mooooomm! Get Babe out of here!" he'd cry, trying to shove the shaggy offender off the field as blocks tumbled down around us.

By the time he reached the age of four—before our odyssey of T-ball, peanut ball, rec ball, and All-Star ball began—Evan was leading us out into the backyard to play wiffle ball. Home plate was a car mat in front of the flower box, first base was under the maple tree, second in front of the forsythia bush, and third beside the garage. The pitcher's mound was a worn spot in the grass behind a raised tree root.

Somehow, with just two or three players, we'd people the entire field and fill the batter's box. As pitchers, we threw heat, and as batters, we knocked bullets into the neighbor's yard. We'd shake off signals from invisible catchers and bellow the umpire's calls. Phantom infielders caught pop-ups and turned athletic double plays, while shadowy outfielders dove for line drives. We'd mimic the intricate signs of the third base coach and, flailing our arms, windmill in the scoring runs.

One afternoon, it was just Evan and me out on our homemade field. It was Evan's favorite team, the Yankees, versus my anonymous sucker team offered up as the sacrifice of the day. No surprise—every one of my batters went down while Evan's boys in pinstripes rounded the bases in triumphant home-run trots. As we began a middle inning with the Yankees in the field, Evan took the mound while I stepped into the batter's box.

Now, I'm not a fearsome batter by any means—I'm lucky to make any contact at all, even on a good day. This time, I whiffed a few, as usual, but finally Evan lobbed a nice, slow arcing ball in my general direction. I took a whack and the ball flew off my bat straight at Evan.

THWACK! The ball hit him hard in the arm.

"Evan!" I cried. "Are you okay? Are you hurt?" I dropped the bat and ran the few steps out to the mound.

I rubbed Evan's arm, now reddening from the impact, and cooed my motherly coos, while he stood silently; ready, I was sure, to burst into tears. Instead, he wheeled around, and without saying a word— *Uh oh, he's mad at me!*—he marched over to first base. He bent over, picked up the ball and brought it back to the mound. He touched the ball to my arm.

"You're out, Mom," he said.

Tagged out while just being a mom! The injustice of it! But the late afternoon sun glinted through the maple leaves, its rays igniting my son's beautiful blond head and pooling in his serious blue eyes as he waited for me to slink back to the dugout in defeat. I laughed. It really *was* a beautiful day for baseball. And it has been ever since.

Nancy B. Kennedy lives in Hopewell, New Jersey, with her husband, John, and their son, Evan. She is the author of three books in the Miracles & Moments of Grace series. Other books to her credit include a book of weight loss success stories and two books of children's science activities. She also writes articles and essays for books, magazines, and newspapers when she's not in the stands cheering for her son's team. Visit her website at www. nancybkennedy.com.

30

A Miracle Baby

Lynn Ely

Newtown, Pennsylvania

My daughter is bright—she was in the gifted program, won academic awards, graduated at the top of her class. She is in college now, majoring in math and physics. She plays field hockey and is an accomplished musician.

It makes me shudder to think that we were advised to end my pregnancy.

Rebecca is our third child. I had a really rough time during my first pregnancy. I developed toxemia, a severe pregnancy-induced hypertension. A month before my due date, my blood pressure shot up so high my doctors decided to induce me. In the operating room, my kidneys began to shut down and I was in danger of having a stroke, so they performed an emergency C-section. My son was in the neonatal intensive care for a month, with a feeding tube and an oxygen tent; but in the end, he was fine.

During my second pregnancy, doctors monitored me closely and both my pregnancy and delivery went smoothly.

Even so, because of the risks, my doctors advised me not to get pregnant again. But I had always envisioned a family of five, so we decided to take a chance. My father is a doctor, so I knew he would keep a close eye on me. And this time, we chose an obstetrics group in Philadelphia so that we could be near Children's Hospital if we encountered serious problems.

As with my second pregnancy, I was monitored throughout. I did have high blood pressure, although not as severe as before. I had ultrasounds every few weeks.

After one ultrasound, the doctor asked my husband and me to accompany him to his office. It wasn't a doctor I knew, and I had a hard time understanding his accent.

"We've seen something that concerns us," he began. "The baby's brain is enlarged, and we see water on the brain. We also have a concern about the brain stem."

"This baby is likely to be severely brain damaged at birth. It is probable the child will not survive beyond a month, but if it does, it will almost certainly have to be institutionalized."

I sat frozen as the doctor continued.

"We feel strongly that, given the likely outcome, you should terminate this pregnancy. It would not be a difficult procedure. As you consider this, keep in mind that you are young, and you can try again."

At these words, I went numb.

Once we left the doctor's office, I called my parents. I was so devastated I couldn't even speak. I sobbed and sobbed as I tried to get the words out.

Yet even in our despair, my husband and I were angry, affronted by the doctor's cold clinical manner. All I could think was: *This is our child you're talking about!* The doctor's words went through my mind, over and over: *"You can try again."* It was as if he were talking about a burnt cake. *It's okay, dear, just throw it out and try again.*

The doctor's dismissive manner only cemented our resolve to continue the pregnancy. My faith in God was not shaken. If this is what God intended for us, it was his choice. "I will not get up on a table and let you do that to me," I informed my doctors.

After we had undergone counseling for our situation, though, it was hard to stay positive. Doubts assailed me. *Will I be able to care for my child? Is this fair to my other children? Will I be able to continue teaching? Will we lose our house if I'm not working?*

In the midst of all this, my husband was asked to take a job in Boston. I didn't want to leave my doctors, so we decided I would stay and he would commute home on weekends. It was a tough decision, and I was left parenting our two children alone.

In my darkest hours, I struggled to come to terms with what was ahead. I prayed for strength, but other thoughts crept into my mind. "Lord, if it is your will to take this child, help me handle it," I prayed. I didn't want that outcome, but I think I was trying to talk myself into it. It seemed the easiest way out.

In my stronger moments, I prayed that I would be okay with whatever happened.

My doctors wanted me to carry the baby as long as possible, despite the hypertension. I was scheduled for an appointment on March 16, at 37 weeks along. On March 12, though, it began to snow in the Northeast. It snowed for three days. They called it the worst storm of the century—the "Blizzard of '93." Route 95 into Philadelphia was closed. *What if I go into labor now?* I worried.

Eventually, Route 95 reopened, and I battled snow-clogged roads to get to my appointment. Based on their evaluation of my condition, the doctors advised me to remain in the hospital and allow them to induce me.

In Boston, Glenn made his way to Logan Airport, which had just reopened. Thankfully, he was able to catch a flight early the next morning. His plane was stacked up on the runway behind fifteen or twenty other planes waiting for takeoff. At one point, he asked the flight attendant how long until departure. He explained his situation, and the flight attendant passed word along to the pilot, who decided to move things along.

"Folks," he said over the intercom, "we have an expectant father on board, so we've been cleared for takeoff now." The entire plane erupted into cheers!

Several hours after Glenn arrived, they wheeled me into the operating room. Doctors stood all around me, ready to intervene instantly. My labor progressed, and suddenly I heard my baby's cry. "It's a girl!" they announced.

"Can you see anything? Is there anything wrong with her?" I asked, so anxious now.

After examining her, the doctors announced that our baby seemed entirely healthy. "We see none of the problems the ultrasounds showed," they said, a little puzzled. They let me hold her right away, and they kept saying that my baby was just fine. Just fine!

We can't say exactly what the doctors saw in their ultrasounds. We wouldn't let them sedate Becky and do an MRI of her brain, as they wanted to do. All I know is that whatever they saw, God took it away. We call Rebecca our Blizzard Baby, but really we know she was our miracle baby—God's wonderful gift to us.

Lynn Ely and her husband, Glenn, live in Newtown, Pennsylvania, and have three adult children, Brett, Kurt, and Rebecca. Lynn has a master's degree in education and teaches seventh grade for the Council Rock School District in lower Bucks County. She and her husband are active at Grace Point Church in Newtown.

NOTE: Rebecca, the Elys' "Blizzard Baby," has written extensively about her birth story. "Because of my start in life, I have always admired my mom's strength and character. She is such a hero to me," she says. "Clearly, God had a bigger plan for my life, and I am so grateful that I was given the chance to live it."

31

SUNDAY MORNING SLEEP-IN

DANIELLE CORNELIUS
DANVILLE, PENNSYLVANIA

It's 8:22 on a Sunday morning, and here I sit with my hair curled and my makeup on, all ready for church. But my kids are still sleeping, so I guess we're going to be late for church—again. I don't dare wake them. Not me! I learned my lesson long ago.

About two years ago, I was getting our three kids ready for church by myself. This happens pretty often, as my husband is in residency as an orthopedic surgeon for the Air Force and is frequently on call overnight. The service starts at 8 A.M., so I have to keep things moving in order to get to church on time.

At the time, my baby was less than 3 months old, my son was not yet 2, and my daughter was a little over 3 years old. On that Sunday morning, I got myself ready hastily thinking they would wake up at any moment. During the week, they are usually up by 7 A.M. But on this day they slept in.

I sat on the stairs trying to decide what to do. Wake them? Go to church late? Not go at all? I had been alone all weekend and really needed the company of my church family—adults to talk to!—so I decided to wake them.

Big mistake! Everyone was grumpy and had an opinion about their Sunday attire. Ella didn't want to wear the dress I put out for her, and my son wouldn't put on his pants.

"I want to wear *this*!" Ella whined, yanking out a checkered skirt, a floral-print dress, and striped tights.

"I want to wear *these* pants!" Peter insisted stubbornly, pointing to a pair of sweatpants.

The clothing battles escalated until there were tears all around.

Meanwhile, the baby was hungry and crying. I tried to get Ella and Peter into their high chairs and eating their breakfasts so I could nurse John. Peter's a messy eater, so it's always a production to get a meal into him.

"Hurry up! Finish up!" I yelled as they dawdled over their yogurt and Cheerios.

After their hurried breakfast, I got the kids cleaned up and the baby dressed and into his carrier. But by now a new battle was brewing. Ella refused to put on the shoes and sweater I'd put out for her.

"I am NOT going to talk about this anymore!" I yelled. "Put your shoes on NOW! Put your sweater on NOW!"

At the same time, Peter started to take off the shoes I'd put on him just minutes ago.

And then Ella said she had to go potty.

Finally, at 8:05 A.M., everyone was dressed and we were ready to head out. I marched them out the back door and toward the car. Our yard is small and very close to our neighbor's house, so I imagine they heard my marching orders as we went.

"Let's go! C'mon! Keep walking!" I shouted, Ella crying as we went.

When we got to the car, I tried to get the baby out of his carrier and into his car seat. In doing so, I hit Peter in the head with the carrier, and then he started crying, too. Beyond frazzled now, I held back tears of frustration and anger as I struggled to get the three of them buckled in.

All of a sudden, Peter stopped crying and, as calm as could be, he looked up at me.

"Mom, where are we going again?" he asked sweetly.

"To CHURCH! We are going to CHURCH!" I yelled, loud enough for the whole neighborhood to hear. And I slammed the car door.

I got into the driver's seat and slumped over the wheel, my response to Peter echoing in my head. Suddenly, it hit me what I had been doing. I had been shouting at my children for a full thirty minutes, showing not one iota of kindness or patience. I hadn't paused for even one second to ask God to help me get my kids out the door in a calm and loving manner.

What was I teaching my children about being joyful in all circumstances—me, the mom who was yelling all the way to church? Nothing! In fact, if anything, my shameful display was showing them that Sunday morning—the morning that starts our day of worship— is truly the most awful morning of the week.

I am the worst mother on the planet! I thought as I replayed the morning in my head. I turned around to face my children, and, with tears in my eyes, I asked their forgiveness for how I had treated them that morning.

As we headed out, I decided that from then on, I was not going to worry about being late for church, or about what anyone thought of us for being late. Trying to get three small children out the door by 8 A.M. is no easy task, and I resolved to give us all some leeway.

These days, we do what we can to ease our Sunday mornings. We set clothes out the night before. I coach the children on what will be expected of them the next morning. I get up early to get myself ready. I hand out yogurt tubes and baggies of cereal for them to eat on the way to church. Sunday mornings have gone much more smoothly in our house since that fateful day. We are all more ready to worship.

So, here I sit at 8:22, all alone and ready for church. I guess it'll just be Sunday school for us today.

Danielle Cornelius lives with her husband, Andrew, in Danville, Pennsylvania, with their three children, Ella, Peter, and John. She has worked as a substitute teacher, in retail, and at a treatment center for foster children. She volunteered for many years with Youth for Christ and has gone to India, Africa, and Mexico on mission trips. At the urging of her mom, Paula, Danielle blogs at Life from a Mom in a Small Town (www. adepcornelius.blogspot.com).

32

A Prayer for Mama's Toes

Sophie Hudson

Birmingham, Alabama

One day a month or so ago, my son Alex and I were in Publix, and completely out of the blue, he asked me if he will go to heaven one day.

Because I was a little distracted by the fact that at some point pot roasts have started to cost about the same as a cute pair of shoes from Target, I sort of off-handedly replied, "Well, yes, buddy, if you have asked Jesus into your heart, then yes, you will go to heaven."

And then Alex got very quiet. After about a full minute of deep soul searching, he screamed, "JEEEEEEEEEEEE-SUS! COME INTO MY HEART!" right there next to the pot roasts. Only, he said it not like he recognized his fallen heart's need for a Savior but more like he was aggravated with Jesus for not sharing his toys.

So while I wasn't completely sure that the little man was clear on some of the more fundamental doctrinal issues, I was entirely certain that Jesus had good reason to take issue with his *tone*.

About five minutes later, I was seized by toe cramps, of all things—toe cramps so severe that I could not imagine that my left foot would ever function properly again—and I told the little man that I had to stop for a second before the pain made my knees buckle. He responded by saying, "Mama, I would like to tell a prayer for you."

I said that would be wonderful, so we bowed our heads right there in front of the dairy case, and he put his hand on my shoulder.

"Dear God," he said. "Please help Mama's toes to feel better in Publix so that she can wear her shoe. In Jesus' name. Amen."

He was so deeply sincere about the whole thing that I wondered for a split second if his profession of faith over in the meat department wasn't the real deal after all.

I'll probably never know exactly what was going on in Alex's heart and mind that day in the grocery store, but I do know that he's been chock-full of curiosity ever since. We've spent the last few weeks talking through all sorts of questions that a 4-year-old would ask about God. While part of me thinks that four is too young for a child to have any real grasp of sin and sacrifice and atonement and resurrection, a much bigger part of me knows that there is no faith as simple and profound as the faith of a child.

I also know that this is the time for us to plant those seeds of faith and water them as much as we possibly can so that the little man's roots will grow deep, so that one day he will be able to grasp, as Paul wrote, "how wide and long and high and deep is the love of Christ and to know this love that surpasses knowledge—that he may be filled to the measure of all the fullness of God."

And so, we answer Alex's questions. We talk about God. We talk about the joys of knowing him, of serving him, of trusting him. We pray that he sees evidence of those joys as he watches his mama and daddy work out their faith every single day.

It has been, quite simply, one of the sweetest times of my
whole life.

Before Alex was born, I imagined that this child whose face I had not
yet seen would sit with me at a desk while I carefully read passages of
Scripture aloud. Everything would be perfectly orderly; I would teach
with care while my child listened attentively. Then we would clasp our
hands together and begin the walk toward faith with lockstep precision,
only stopping long enough for him to surrender to whatever calling God
might have on his life.

Because I wasn't idealistic or anything.

But the reality, as anybody with a little one knows, is absolutely
nothing like that. The daily process of teaching and leading a precious
little heart is about as methodical as herding a room full of cats. And
you know what else? It is hard. On every single level. So much of parenting uncovers our own imperfections, and we are constantly being
humbled, broken, and refined in our own lives while we try to nurture
the little lives that have been entrusted to us.

Did I mention that it's hard?

There are days when I'm really disappointed in myself as a mother.
I get so tired of struggling to balance the things I need to do with
the things I want to do. As a result of that, I am confronted with the
reality of my selfishness over and over again. It's a mighty good thing
indeed that I don't have to parent in my own strength, because I'll tell
you right now that I couldn't do it. I wouldn't last a day.

But the rewards of parenting? They really are huge. They're
immeasurable. They're eternal. And the longer I'm a mama, the more
I find that the most teachable moments in terms of faith don't require
much organization or planning on my part. They don't necessarily
happen while we're sitting in a church service or when we're reviewing

memory verses with great intention, though certainly, I believe that God uses those things.

For me, the most breathtaking moments—the times when my husband and I are both able to share our faith with the most sincerity and transparency—are when Alex picks up a maple leaf from the ground and then says, with wonder, "God made this!" Or when he runs into the house after being outside and says, "Mama! I missed you! And I talked to Jesus while I played!" Or when he's sick with a stomach virus and says, through his tears, "Mama? Will you always take care of me? Will God always take care of me?"

Or even when he puts his hand on my shoulder in the middle of a crowded grocery store and prays for my toe cramps while we stand next to six different brands of sour cream.

In many ways, motherhood is absolutely nothing like I imagined, but so much more than I expected. And for me, right now, the greatest joy is sharing the Greatest Joy with a 4-year-old who may get a little cloudy on the theological details, but whose heart is wide open.

I cannot imagine any greater privilege.

Sophie Hudson writes about the funny, joy-filled moments of everyday life on her blog, BooMama (www.boomama.net). She contributes to the entertainment section of The Pioneer Woman website and the LifeWay Women All Access blog. Also a regular contributor to HomeLife *magazine, Sophie has traveled with Compassion International on blogger trips to Uganda and Ecuador. Sophie lives with her husband and son in Birmingham, Alabama, where they are members of the Church at Brook Hills. "A Prayer for Mama's Toes" was originally published on the BooMama blog as "To Know this Love That Surpasses Knowledge" (October 23, 2007) and adapted with permission. She is currently working on her first book,* Cut the Sweet: Southern Stories of Faith, Family and Fifteen Pounds of Bacon, *to be released in June 2013 by Tyndale House Publishers. Sophie plans to sleep sometime in 2014—and she can hardly wait.*

33

MY SMALLEST DREAM

DÉA VIOLA
ESSEX COUNTY, NEW JERSEY

Where there is great love there are always miracles.

WILLA CATHER

At the moment of my fourth child's birth—a breathtaking moment that is such a precious gift to a mother—I regret to this day that could not look at her face. I was too afraid.

I believe that all babies are miracles, and I clung to this belief even after I had two difficult miscarriages. Soon after my second miscarriage, I found out I was expecting again. I did not tell a soul, not even my husband.

As I entered my sixth week of pregnancy, the doctor said everything looked good. It was time for an ultrasound. I was so excited! I had seen the black, empty screen of two heartbreaking ultrasounds, but now I thought, *Could it be? Is it really going to be OK this time?*

During the exam, the technician and my doctor were uncomfortably silent. Afterward, I got dressed and followed the doctor into her office.

"Given your hormone levels, we should have seen something," she said.

I went home in tears. I felt that if I could not hold this baby, my heart would be broken forever. I picked up my guitar and wrote a song willing my baby to hang on for just one week until I could see the tiny heartbeat on the screen. I called my lullaby, "My Smallest Dream."

But still my spirit was broken. I knelt down, and for the first time in my life, I prayed with all my might. On my knees, I begged God to grant me my wish.

A week later, I went back for a second ultrasound. To our surprise, there it was—the heartbeat! What a beautiful sound! The most beautiful sound I had ever heard. My baby had made it!

Confident now, I went home and shared the news. My husband and I were jubilant!

But our joy did not last. At eighteen weeks, the results of my amniocentesis were devastating. My baby, which I now knew was a girl, had an abnormality of the X chromosome known as Turner syndrome. It's a syndrome whose severity is not known until the baby's birth.

Upon hearing the news, I literally dropped to the floor. I could not see—I thought I had gone blind.

Turner syndrome sometimes presents itself in the form of missing cells. In my baby's case, a part of her X chromosomes were not evident, indicating she had a form of Turner syndrome known as "mosaicism." That word described how my heart felt—my "mosaic heart" had broken into millions of tiny pieces.

I was paralyzed with fear. I felt completely helpless—unable to help my baby, unable to help myself. *Maybe I should just terminate the pregnancy,* I thought.

I hated myself and my body. Even worse, I hated God. It was the biggest revelation I had ever experienced. I always thought that I had faith. But there it was, the real truth about me: When faced with adversity, I had no faith. It was an ugly discovery.

I went to the genetic counseling appointment with my husband, and we fought all the way there.

"What do you want me to do?" I cried. "Do we have the right to bring this baby into the world? Will other kids laugh at her, mock her deformities? Will our other children be laughed at, too?"

My husband's answer was simple.

"I just want my daughter," he answered me.

Silently, we held hands and walked into the office.

The counselor gave us the possible scenarios. The baby might not survive the pregnancy, she said. If she does live, the syndrome can be as mild as causing her to be shorter than average and have extra skin on the neck, or suffer from frequent ear infections. But it could also be so severe as to cause heart and skeletal defects and kidney problems. The ear infections could lead to deafness. Infertility was almost certain.

Hearing that news, even the more dire possibilities, I knew what to do: I was willing to take a chance. Yes, my baby's life was worth it! Almost 40 years ago, I reasoned, I was saved by the unconditional love of a woman who was willing to adopt two gravely ill girls—my twin sister and me—from an orphanage in Brazil.

God has given my baby to me, and if he wants her back, he will have to get her himself! That's what I decided. God had chosen me to be this baby's mother, not the person who chooses whether she lives or dies. Immediately, I felt the weight lift off my burdened soul.

Even so, I was still scared and sad. I prayed every day on my knees and then cried myself to sleep. With all my heart, I wanted a healthy baby, but I didn't see how God could grant me my wish. I sang my baby's lullaby every day. My lullaby became my prayer, my voice, the link between God and my daughter. "Stay with me," I sang.

Just a few more days,

'Til I see you,

'Til I can feel your tiny heart.

You are my love,

And my smallest dream.

It was a Saturday morning at 7 A.M.—April Fool's Day, no less!—when I first felt twinges. My due date was more than two weeks away, but soon enough the twinges turned to pressure, and we headed for the hospital. The pressure quickly turned to pain, and a half an hour later, before a doctor could even get to me, my baby was born.

This is the moment that I missed, the moment every mother longs for, the moment she first sees her beautiful child. But I didn't have the courage. I looked away.

A few minutes later, the neonatologist came into the room. I held my breath—and he gave us the thumbs up! My baby had absolutely no sign of Turner syndrome! I finally held her when she was ten minutes old. She was rosy, and so, so beautiful! I was in awe.

At my baby's first checkup, my pediatrician held out the lab report, and smiling, she said, "Everything looks normal!" I covered my face, and I just could not stop my tears.

My 4-year-old son Thomas flung open the door to the office and ran out into the waiting room.

"My baby sister isn't sick anymore!" he yelled to the astonished occupants.

Giuliana Sofia Viola is now 7 years old. She is one hundred percent healthy. On my most desperate days, when I begged God to give me a perfect baby, I did not come close to what my Giuliana Sofia is today. We still cannot explain what happened. The doctors say they have never seen this happen. She is our little miracle.

Yet no matter how perfect or imperfect my baby, I would still call her a miracle, for all babies are miracles. For me, the true miracle of her birth is the chance I was given to take this journey of faith with God. When I was fearful, he comforted me. In my weakness, he gave me strength. I grew spiritually in ways that are beyond words. My life is forever changed. I want to tell the whole world about my smallest—and most perfect!—dream.

Déa Viola is the mother of five children, Maria, John, Thomas, Giuliana Sofia, and Daniel. She and her husband, Daniel, live with their family in Essex County, New Jersey. She is a professional singer and dancer; she danced with the Joffrey Ballet and the Alvin Ailey American Dance Theater and was a stand-in for the tango scene in the movie Scent of a Woman. *Currently, she sings with a rock band in Montclair, New Jersey. Her company, The Baby Flamingo Co. (www.thebabyflamingoco.com), has won many awards, including a PTPA (Parent Tested, Parent Approved™) Media Award and The Next Big Zing™ Award, both in 2011. In 2010, she won a Huggies® MomInspired™ Grant Program Award for her creation, The Mama Taco Towel,™ a hands-free baby bath towel. The lyrics from "My Smallest Dream" are reprinted with permission. © Copyright Déa Viola 2008–11. All Rights Reserved.*

34

BUNK BED BLUNDER

ANNMARIE B. TAIT

CONSHOHOCKEN, PENNSYLVANIA

The heart of a mother is a deep abyss at the bottom of which
you will always find forgiveness.

HONORÉ DE BALZAC

For a full twenty minutes I begged my older sister to trade bunks with me for one measly night. I just had to know the thrill of sleeping in the top bunk, or die of disappointment. Life is just that dramatic when you're 8 years old.

My sister, the self-appointed president of the "Do-Gooders Club," was not so all-fired sure that this was such a great idea. After all, more than once Mom had warned me to stay away from the top bunk.

Eventually my sister gave in to me on the pinky promise that I would never, ever, as long as I drew breath, speak a word to Mom about our shenanigans.

"Deal!" I said, with a grin that stretched from one earlobe to the other.

After supper, I attacked my homework with the dedication of a
Rhodes scholar and the speed of a gazelle. With that behind me, I
ripped off my clothes, jumped into the tub, then into my jammies, and
then into Daddy's comfy chair. I waited, and waited, and *waited* for
Ricky Nelson to sing "Travelin' Man" or some other hit that signaled the
end of the *Ozzie and Harriet* show and the start of my bedtime escapade.
Soon, I was bounding up the living room steps two at a time.

"You didn't forget, did you?" I asked my sister.

"No," she said, "But, I still don't think it's a good idea."

"I don't care!" I shot back in a panic. "You promised!"

All evening, I imagined the top bunk bed as a flying carpet upon
which I could dash off to Disneyland, a cowboy ranch, the circus,
or anywhere I wanted to go. I imagined it as a tree house, a magical
flying unicorn, a hot air balloon like the one I'd seen in the *Wizard
of Oz*.

One thing was for sure, I'd never get anywhere unless I got myself
up into that top bunk with the lights out before my two oldest sisters
came to bed, found me out, and blew the lid off my little caper.

Our bunk beds, purchased at the local Army Navy Surplus store,
were made of gray steel that Mom had painted white. They were not
equipped with an adorable little ladder like the maple bunk beds I
saw advertised in the Sears catalog. Launching to the top was strictly
up to the strength and dexterity of the occupant.

To get me up there, my sister stood bent over with her fingers
laced together. I stepped into the cradle of her hands with one foot,
grabbed the top bunk, and then hoisted myself up while she pushed
me at the same time.

Hardly had I made to the land of Oz on my flying magical unicorn,
though, when, wouldn't you know it? I fell fast asleep.

Sometime after midnight, I woke up and realized a trip to the bathroom was in order. With a sleepy yawn, I threw back the covers, swung my legs over the side, and stepped off into thin air, plummeting to the floor with a loud thud.

Mom and Daddy ran to our bedroom with breakneck speed. Daddy picked me up off the floor and my sister scooted over in the lower bunk. Then Daddy gently put me down next to her.

"I'm so sorry," was all I could say. My mother bent over and kissed me and asked if I was all right.

"Fine. I'm fine. I'm so sorry!" I answered. She just whispered, "Go to sleep now."

Mom didn't scold me. She never so much as reminded me of her warning to stay away from the top bunk.

When the commotion settled down, my sister asked me if I was really okay.

"I'm not sure," I said. "My arm hurts a little. I'll probably be okay in the morning." She drifted off to sleep, and I lay there filled with shame. My arm throbbed, and I couldn't close my eyes the rest of the night.

As daybreak approached, I knew I wouldn't be going to school that day. I woke my sister and asked her to get Mom for me.

My mother sat down on the bed next to me, and the tears I had held in all night now flowed freely.

"I don't think I can move my arm," I said, between sniffles.

"Why didn't you tell me last night?" she said, smoothing my long brown hair away from my eyes.

"Because . . . I'm so ashamed." By now I was sobbing.

Mom didn't drive and Daddy had long since left for work. So, after she dressed me, we trudged three blocks to the bus stop. The bus was crowded. Mom stood next to me with her arm around my shoulder to steady me as best she could as the bus rumbled down the street.

When we arrived in the emergency room, I was whisked off for an X-ray. As we waited together for the results, she put her arm around me and assured me that everything would be okay. The ice pack the nurse gave me kept sliding off my arm, but my mother held it in place and spoke softly to keep me calm.

When all was said and done, my wrist was fractured. When we left, I was sporting a plaster cast from my knuckles clear up over my elbow.

On the way home, we got off the bus two stops early and went into the five-and-ten. The butter pecan ice cream they served at the lunch counter was top notch and we ordered two cones. Somewhere between licks, I summoned the courage to ask my mother why I didn't get in trouble for sleeping in the top bunk.

"You didn't need any lecture from me," Mom said. "Your conscience took care of that. What you needed was someone's hand to hold, someone's shoulder to cry on, and someone to buy you an ice cream cone when the whole thing was behind you."

Now, when it is on the tip of my tongue to say "I told you so" to someone who is already suffering the consequences of a poor choice, I remember that special day with my mother. I think twice, and then I suggest that we go get an ice cream cone.

Annmarie B. Tait lives in Conshohocken, Pennsylvania, with her husband, Joe Beck. Annmarie is published in various anthologies including Chicken Soup for the Soul, Patchwork Path, the HCI Ultimate series and Reminisce magazine. Annmarie has been nominated for a 2013 Pushcart Prize for her story "Her Eye on the Sparrow," which was published in Thin Threads: Moms and Grandmas *(Kiwi, 2011). In addition to writing, she also enjoys cooking, sewing, and crocheting.*

35

GRACE FOR THIS DAY

SUSAN ETOLE JONES
CLEARWATER COUNTY, MINNESOTA

Do not worry about tomorrow,
for tomorrow will worry about itself.
Each day has enough trouble of its own.

MATTHEW 6:34

How I wish that I could you tell you that this is a story of great faith, but it is not. It is, however, a story of great faithfulness. The faithfulness of a great God.

My story begins on an August Saturday in Montana's Big Sky Country. My husband had recently flown to Texas for his officer's training in the Air Force. My brother, my parents, and I were on the road, halfway home from a vacation in Minnesota and headed for Washington State. They were in the front seat; I was lying across the back seat. The year was 1967, and seat belts were still a novelty in all but the newest cars.

Suddenly, we were enveloped in a cacophonous whirlwind of noise and dirt and broken glass. We had been struck nearly head-on by a driver passing illegally on a hill. The impact of the collision threw me to the floor. In that split second, my life forever changed. A spinal cord injury left me paralyzed from the chest down.

I was 22 years old.

During the next hour, we waited for the ambulance along with a middle-aged couple and their daughter who came to help. They attended to my father, who sat in a ditch, dazed from hitting the windshield. They spoke reassuringly to my mother, who remained in the front seat with a severely broken arm.

My brother, who appeared to be okay although shaken, remained by me. As he brushed broken glass from my face, I told him repeatedly that my legs felt as though they were bent backward. He assured me that was not the case. But from his experience as an ambulance driver, he knew then what I didn't.

"Just pray, Susie," he said quietly. "Just pray."

Eventually, I was moved into a waiting ambulance. I caught a glimpse of the family that had stayed with us and was able to thank them. We never knew their name. I suspect it was "Saint" something.

An hour is a very long time in the back of an ambulance. The game warden, who had heard the crash, rode in the back with me. He asked if he could cut away my clothes; he thought it might help me be more comfortable, to breathe easier. I declined. Later, in the emergency room, my favorite blue jeans and blouse would be cut away.

In the emergency room, they asked if I had insurance, what my religion was, how they could contact my husband. I told them that they couldn't. That he had just enlisted in the Air Force and was only to be contacted in case of an emergency. It took them several hours to convince me that this was indeed an emergency.

Two days later, on August 28, my husband and I observed our second anniversary in the intensive care unit. I had had surgery to fuse the vertebrae in my back with bone taken from my hip. I was on a Stryker frame, which they turned every two hours. I was either face up or face down. Either way, I hurt.

I was also three months pregnant.

When the doctor came into the ICU after my surgery, he delivered the somber news that I would never walk again.

"That's okay," I told him. "God will take care of me." I knew—my heart knew—that God answered prayer, that I would be healed. The tears in his eyes said otherwise.

The days passed. The weeks passed. The months passed. I didn't understand why my feeling didn't return. Why the paralysis contin-ued. It wasn't so much that I believed in healing. It was that I believed in answered prayer. And God always answered prayer. *Didn't he?*

The doctor thought I hadn't understood him when he'd given me the news. I thought he didn't understand about God.

I spent the next six months in the hospital. Six months of pain. Six months of blood transfusions. Six months of tears. For six long months, we waited for the birth of our child. My husband was given a humanitarian assignment at nearby Great Falls Air Force Base, and my mother remained with us.

There were moments of grace. The nurses became my friends. They brought me a homemade Thanksgiving dinner, and later, a Christmas tree that they decorated. The doctor's children sang Christmas carols for me. A shy orderly brought flowers to keep my spirits up.

Early on a February Sunday morning, our son was born. He was beautiful. Perfect in every way. And he was a redhead to boot.

Four weeks later, my son went home with my husband and my mother. I didn't. I had yet to learn to sit and balance in a wheelchair, how to transfer off and on a bed and into a car, and myriads of other daily living tasks.

To say my heart was broken the day my son went home without me would be an understatement. I felt betrayed by God. He had let me be a mother to a wonderful baby boy, and yet someone else would take him home.

I was his mother. I longed to be with him.

One month later, I did go home. To a home I had not yet seen. To a city we had not lived in until my husband was assigned there. But I went home to a healthy baby boy. To a mother who, with my father's blessing, was graciously helping to care for him, although it meant a lengthy separation for my parents. And to a life that had to be learned anew.

We were a bewildered bunch. It was a bitter pill to swallow, not being able to care for my baby the way I wanted to. When I first came home, I could not hold Jay or feed him. Although I had the use of my arms, I didn't have the strength to sit up. But gradually, we made our way. My mother stayed with us for nineteen months while we adjusted to our new life.

In the midst of our wilderness, I can say that God gave us grace for every day. You probably know the story of the Israelites, how they wandered in the wilderness for forty years. How God provided manna from heaven for them to eat, one day at a time. Well, that is how my journey has gone. I have been given manna, one day at a time.

My doctor once told me that I'd be a bitter old woman if I didn't live that way, that one-day-at-a-time way. He was right. Forty-four years later, he is still right.

Time after time, my faith has faltered and fallen. My faith knees have been scraped and bruised. Theologies about this, that, and the other thing have come and gone. My husband is no longer my husband. My wheelchair remains.

But this one thing I know. God is always faithful. Always good. Always love. He loved me the day I was thrown from the back seat of a car. He loved me the day a doctor told me I would never walk again. He loved me the day my baby went home without me. He loved me by giving me a son, now grown, who along with his wife and son are blessings to me always. God loves me. I've learned this. One day at a time.

Susan Etole Jones lives in Clearwater County, Minnesota, on land that her grandfather homesteaded in 1896, when he emigrated from Sweden. Her son, Jay, lives nearby with his wife and son in the home that Susan's parents built when they retired and moved back to Minnesota, a lifelong dream of theirs. Susan is a photographer and has worked as a church secretary. Visit her blog Just . . . a Moment at www.susan-moment.blogspot.com. "Grace for This Day" first appeared on February 12, 2012, as "Faithful" on Jennifer Duke Lee's blog, Getting Down With Jesus, and was adapted with permission.

36

DARE TO BE DIFFERENT

GINGER LYONS

SPOKANE, WASHINGTON

"Congratulations, your son has the biggest head ever born to a woman in this hospital!"

This is what I remember about the moment that my sweet Colton made his entrance into the world. The nurse went on with her assessment of ears, toes, fingers, and nose, but I will never forget her comment about Colton's head.

"A child with a melon like that must be extraordinarily smart!" my husband chimed in.

My beautiful, nine-pound baby boy was the envy of everyone I knew. He slept through the night and woke up every morning with a smile on his face. He never liked mind-numbing games like patty cake and didn't care to respond to the boring questions Dora the Explorer asked.

He was, however, in jubilation just to lie in the grass or watch the blades of a ceiling fan turn for hours. One day when he was about a year old, he pushed his saucer walker over to a light switch and began turning it on and off. He was ecstatic!

After that, Colton's life centered around the wonder of the light bulb. I dreaded taking him anywhere in public for fear that somewhere, sometime a light bulb might be burnt out. At the age of two, he could tell a person—and he would!—that one of the three hundred lights over our heads at Walmart was burnt out. He'd insist that I alert someone about the problem—and demand that it be fixed.

"Ummm, excuse me," I'd start to say to the poor, trapped employee. "Did you know that you have a burnt-out light bulb over in the toy aisle?"

It was exhausting for me as a mother. We had to make nightly sweeps of the house to check whether any light bulbs were burnt out or needed to be turned off. Annoying though that was, my husband and I considered it simply part of Colton's daily routine and nothing more. In all other ways, Colton was just like other children.

However, at some point, Colton's speech began to decline rapidly. Although his vocabulary had been completely in step with other children his age, within weeks he lost the ability to say more than thirty words. Eventually, at 30 months, "star" was the only word he could say.

We took Colton for evaluations with the ear, nose, and throat specialists and enrolled him in speech therapy classes. Tests soon showed that he was unable to hear anything out of his left ear and only about 10 percent out of his right. We scheduled surgery to implant ear tubes into our toddler's tiny, fragile ears.

At the same time, I met with a public health nurse and enrolled Colton in a local early intervention program for children with speech difficulties. There, he began to meet weekly with speech, occupational, and physical therapists in a fun and motivational environment.

Colton's progress was slow, though, because week after week the administrator failed to replace one, tiny burnt-out light bulb in the middle of the classroom ceiling. Predictably, therapists were soon talking with us about our son's "fixation."

Frustrated, I began to come down hard on Colton. "Do not talk about light bulbs!" I'd admonish him, and I'd punish him when he did.

A few weeks into the classes, my husband and I were asked to meet with the therapists. As we walked in and sat down with the group of five adults, I immediately sensed a problem. This, I could tell, was an intervention.

A woman in the group handed us stacks of papers and telephone numbers and over the next thirty minutes shared with us what it was like to have an autistic child. *What did she just say?* I thought when I heard the word "autistic." I was stunned. I wanted to run out of the room screaming. I wanted to go to Colton and hug him tight.

"Colton most probably has high-functioning Asperger's, which is a variant of autism," she went on. I didn't hear anything after that.

After the meeting, I became obsessed with autism and Asperger's. I spent all of my waking hours on the computer reading articles and visiting autism chat rooms. I served dinner to my husband every evening with a new stack of evidence that proved or disproved Colton's "condition." We disagreed on everything, fought constantly.

We picked apart everything that our poor child said and did. I raised my voice any time Colton said anything about a light bulb or a vacuum cleaner, for now his obsession had grown to include that appliance as well.

Yet as Colton's mom, I just didn't see the same child the therapists saw. Yes, he had a speech delay and the fixation on one subject that characterizes Asperger's, but he didn't have any of the other characteristics. He had no trouble interacting with other people, understanding social cues, making eye contact, playing with other children, and talking conversationally. In fact, I couldn't get him to stop talking for more than thirty seconds!

Confused, I called my cousin, who is a psychologist. She confirmed the characteristics I had read about, yet almost nothing she said fit Colton's story.

"Maybe Colton's just extraordinarily smart," she suggested at last.

Yes! Finally! Words that fit.

With the help of ear tubes, Colton's speech was completely restored within months. Now, at the age of five, he has play dates with friends, interacts with his little brother, and can say anything with ease.

Instead of fearing our son's interests, we have decided to encourage them. Rather than criticize his differences, we reward them. I search the internet for pictures to add to Colton's bulging notebook of ceiling fan photos. We've given him battery-operated light bulbs and an electrical kit. We bought him a vacuum cleaner for Christmas. Lately, he has branched out into rechargeable candles and anatomy books. We even fought our way through the Disney hierarchy to get to someone who would listen to Colton's ideas for making WALL-E a better robot!

My journey through mothering has taught me to embrace my child and all that comes with him. God made us all different, and I want to celebrate Colton's differences. Does every 5-year-old have a body parts placemat? Probably not. But sometimes, it's so boring to follow the crowd.

Ginger Lyons and her husband, Lance, live in Spokane, Washington, and have two boys, Colton and Dylan. Ginger spent four years in the United

States Coast Guard serving in law enforcement and search and rescue. On July 16, 1996, she was among the first rescuers to reach the scene of the TWA Flight 800 explosion off the coast of New York that killed all 239 people on board. She has written for United States Coast Guard publications and was a restaurant reviewer for Dan's Papers, *a newspaper in New York's Hamptons resort area.*

37

THE DIRTY DAYS OF SUMMER

EUGENE, OREGON

Summer afternoon . . .
the two most beautiful words in the English language.

HENRY JAMES

I love summer; I love the changes it brings. I bask in the sunshine, glory in the green of the grass and the beautiful blue of the sky, and delight in hearing the songbirds return after a wet, drizzly Oregon winter. Everyone seems to be smiling. For me, summer is just a glimpse into how great God's plan was for creation before we did that whole apple thing.

In some ways, being a mother is easier in the summer. The days seem to speed by. No one is begging to watch a movie or play a game on the computer. In the summer, my three boys are more interested in the endless adventures to be had outside around our farm.

The downside of summer is that my kids get so dirty! They bound out of bed and then out into our little piece of Eden—heading straight for the dirt, the sand box, the garden, the woods, or a very sought-after dip in the river. They run barefoot in the grass, mow the lawn with Grandpa, wrestle with our yellow lab, weed the garden with me, create roads for their trucks in the rocks of the gravel driveway, eat fresh berries, and have epic battles in their play fort. Then they run with sunny exuberance straight back into my white-carpeted house—with filthy dirty feet.

I try to keep the damage to a minimum. I've placed five area rugs strategically around the living room and have instructed my sons to hop from rug to rug to preserve the carpet. The line of grimy rugs adds to the hodgepodge nature of my décor, a look that I like to claim is intentional but is really an outgrowth of necessity. Come September, I lift the rugs and call in the professional carpet cleaners.

One day when our oldest son, Bren, was four he spent a full hour drawing with chalk out on the front porch, engrossed and content. I was glad for his creative play, but meanwhile, his bottom morphed into a repository of dusty hues. The dirty shorts didn't bother me— they're easy to clean—but when those chalky pastels made it into the house on his backside and ended up smeared all over my carpet and furniture, I felt a sudden burst of anger. Sometimes it seems a constant battle, fighting back the chaos that kids innocently trail around behind them.

I struggle as I compare my home to other homes I have been in. Other women seem able to keep their house looking orderly and put together. When I see a house like that, I become motivated. I think, *I could have that perfect home!* I could take control, impose strict rules, expend more energy tidying up. Then I'll have that coffee-table-magazine-worthy House Beautiful, too.

One friend suggested I force my sons to wear their shoes outside and then stand over them at the back door, making sure they take them off there before they come in. I could do this. I could make this my battle to win. It could work.

But then I stop to think of what would be sacrificed were I to become obsessed with cleanliness and order. I remember how fun it was to run in the grass barefoot when I was a child, especially on these glorious, fleeting days of summer. The bliss of an endless sunny day, the freedom from rules, the discoveries of nature, the carefree friend-ships—I remember it all. There was simplicity in the spontaneity and freedom that summer brought.

Am I willing to deny my children these things, all in the name of household order and cleanliness? I breathe deep. No, I find that I just cannot steal these childhood joys from my sons. I relinquish my war on dirt. I choose to hold my desire for perfection loosely.

So, into the house they dash, with blackened feet. I try to grab them at the back door and at least give the soles of their feet a wash in the sink, but I can't always keep up with the in-and-out traffic. And then, sud-denly, I realize I don't want to. There are better ways to be their mother.

Summer is a season, just as these early childhood years are also a season. Amid all the dirt and grime, my three boys are experiencing the pure joy that God once planned for all of creation. And so, day by day, my white carpet gradually devolves into a muddy, indecipherable color. And you know what? I'm okay with that. I've already started saving up for the carpet cleaners.

Rebekah D. Schneiter and her husband, Hans, are the parents of three boys, Bren, Coen, and Aren, who have endless adventures on their farm outside of Eugene, Oregon. For eight years, she has written a parenting column for the Newberg Graphic. *She is also a contributing writer to the* Oregon Women's Report, *has been published by MOPS International, and contributed to* The Things You Would Have Said *project by Jackie Hooper (Hudson Street Press, 2012), a collection of letters chronicling words left unsaid. She has co-authored a book titled* Just Moms: Conveying Justice in an Unjust World *(Barclay Press, 2011). Read more about her outnumbered life at Rebekah-Outnumbered (www.rebekah-outnumbered.blogspot.com).*

38

ANGELS ON THE LOOKOUT

GLYNNIS WHITWER

GLENDALE, ARIZONA

For he will command his angels concerning you
to guard you in all your ways.

PSALM 91:11

I woke up at 4 o'clock on a Saturday morning. No noise disturbed my sleep. No dog licked my face. I just woke up.

It didn't feel like a divine awakening. There was no prompting to do anything special, so I just got up and started my day early.

Around 2 in the afternoon, I started to fade, so I stopped to rest on the couch. My 12-year-old son Robbie snuggled up next to me, and we enjoyed a few quiet moments together.

To explain my exhaustion, I told Robbie how early I'd awakened.

"That's weird, Mom," Robbie said. "I woke up at 4 o'clock too."

"Why didn't you come downstairs?" I asked. "We could have spent the early morning together."

Robbie got very still and silent, and he had an odd look on his face.

"I was afraid to get up," he replied.

I looked fully at Robbie and asked what had frightened him.

"I thought I saw a man sitting in the chair beside my bed," Robbie answered sheepishly, a little embarrassed in the light of day about what had scared him in the dark.

In a moment of divine revelation, and without a pause, I responded, "Robbie, I'm not surprised you saw someone sitting by your bed. As your mother, I've been praying for God to protect you every day. Ever since you were a baby, I've prayed for God to send his biggest, strongest angels to watch over you and your brothers.

"Robbie, I think you got to see an angel this morning."

At my words, relief flooded Robbie's features and together we grinned in delight at what God had allowed him to see.

But Robbie wasn't finished yet. Emboldened by my belief in his story and in his assurance of God's protection, Robbie wanted to share another heavenly sighting with me.

His face changed from the expression of concern I'd seen just a few moments before to one of excitement. He sat up straight and began.

"One night I got up to get a drink, Mom," he said. "I walked into the playroom and saw a man dressed like an Army man. He had on camouflage and was wearing boots. And he was looking out the back window . . . like he was on patrol. I didn't say anything and he never looked at me. I was afraid, so I just snuck back into my bed.

"Mom," he said with awe, "Do you think he was guarding us?"

"Oh, yes, Robbie," I answered. "I'm sure of it."

In that moment, I received an amazing assurance—a stunningly visual confirmation that my prayers as a mother had been heard and answered. It was the kind of assurance that burrows its way deep inside the soul, and I sensed God's delight as he watched understanding wash over me. Robbie and I had been shown a rare glimpse into the heavenly kingdom that surrounds us.

Still, I wasn't surprised that Robbie was a bit unnerved by the sightings. For generations, since the beginning of time really, angels have scared almost everyone who has seen them. And who wouldn't be afraid? You look up, and there's a strange being! Maybe he's glowing with an otherworldly light, or maybe he's transparent. Or maybe, as for Robbie, he just looks like a man in battle fatigues standing guard over sleeping children. Whatever the case, in the Bible, almost every time an angel appears to a human being, the first words out of his mouth are, "Be not afraid."

Perhaps that's why angels choose to remain unseen. And yet I'm confident they have been and continue to be present in my life. I believe they camp around my house because I've asked God for his protection. There's nothing special about me and my request; I'm just a mother who is desperately aware of her inability to protect her children. And I'm a woman who makes a willful choice every day to trust that what God says is true, and that he can do what he says he can do. Thankfully, that includes opening heaven's doors and sending down his unique kind of mother's helper.

I don't know why Robbie has been blessed to see angels guarding him. What I do know is that God cares about the prayers of a mother's heart. And he cares about the faith of a little boy who has experienced God's power in a personal way.

Glynnis Whitwer and her husband, Tod, live in Glendale, Arizona. They have five children, Joshua, Dylan, Cathrine, Robbie, and Ruth. She is on staff with Proverbs 31 Ministries as senior editor of P31 Woman magazine. She is one of the writers of Encouragement for Today, *the* Proverbs 31 Ministries *e-mail devotional reaching over five hundred thousand readers daily. She is the author of several books, including* I Used to Be So Organized *(Leafwood, 2011) and* When Your Child Is Hurting *(Harvest House, 2009). Learn more about Glynnis at her website, www. Glynniswhitwer.com, where she writes about blending peace and productivity in everyday life.*

39

MY LITTLE BIRDIE

NANCY BUTLER
WATERFORD, CONNECTICUT

God couldn't be everywhere, so he created mothers.

YIDDISH PROVERB

As a single parent, it was challenging to raise two girls on my own. I was starting my own business, we were living in a new city, and I didn't have anyone nearby to help me. When I was at work, I felt guilty that I wasn't with my daughters. But when I was with them, I often couldn't put away the work that I needed to do to keep a roof over our heads.

I put some strict household rules in place to ensure that we would operate smoothly as a family. Probably the biggest rule was that you had to pick up after yourself. You leave a room the way you found it. So, for example, if you want to eat in the living room, you use a snack tray, remove all your dishes when you're done, and put the tray back where you found it. I may be a little obsessive about cleanliness, but I just couldn't face coming home to a mess after working all day.

Another hard and fast rule in my home was that my daughters could not have anyone in the house when I was not there. One of my daughters was a teenager and the other a preteen, so I really felt that I had to protect my girls in this way. Because my office was outside of our home, I needed a way to see what was going on at home when I wasn't there—and there was no such thing as a "nanny cam" back then!

I devised a few methods to clue me in as to what went on at home during the day. For example, we had swivel chairs in the kitchen. Before I left for the day, I made sure that all of the chairs faced in the same direction. Because I knew where my children always sat, if one of the chairs was facing another direction, I knew that someone other than my daughters had probably moved it.

In the living room, I found that if I brushed the nap of the fabric of the sofa and chairs in one direction, it was easy to see if someone had sat down. The "butt indents" gave away a lot of information about who had been there!

But the most telling clue involved vacuuming. Before going out for the day, I vacuumed the carpet against the nap and all in one direction, making the pile stand high. If someone walked into the room, I could tell. And of course, different shoe sizes or different treads meant that more than one person had been there.

One day, returning home from work, I checked for footprints in the carpet. It was clear that someone other than my daughters had been in the room. There were large prints and small prints, and in fact, when I looked closely, it appeared that there must have been about three other people in the house that day.

"Was anyone in the house while I was gone today?" I asked my daughter, feigning ignorance.

"No, no one was here, Mom," she answered.

"Well, a little birdie told me you had several people in the house while I was gone," I answered.

"What! What little birdie?" she asked, shocked that I knew her secret.

And of course, I would not tell her.

Caught in her deception, my daughter finally admitted to me that one of her girlfriends and two of their guy friends were "keeping her company" while I was out. I reminded her of the rules of the house, and then I restricted her activities for two weeks for breaking the rules and another two weeks for lying to me.

People may find my methods a little over the top, but I had long-term goals in mind for my children. I wanted them to have opportunities to express themselves and feel proud of their accomplishments. I wanted them to have fun, but also to grow into responsible adults. No matter how difficult my job as a single parent, I didn't want to focus solely on the moment. In order to be able to focus on the future together, I needed our household to run smoothly from day to day. My daughters never could figure out how my little birdie worked. I never confessed my tricks, and they're in their 40s now. So, my darling daughters, if you're reading this, this is how I knew.

Nancy Butler lives in Waterford, Connecticut, with her husband, Jim. She was a personal financial planner and asset manager for twenty-five years before selling her business. After practicing some traditional and not-so-traditional methods of managing her children, her business, and her life, she became a business and personal life coach. She speaks on both motivational and practical topics and blogs at her company's website, Above All Else (www.aboveallelse.org). Her two daughters are now grown and live in Florida and Connecticut. Nancy's first book, Above All Else: Success in Life and Business, *was released by Annotation Press in September 2012.*

40

THE RED APPLE

JENNIFER DUKES LEE

INWOOD, IOWA

So much about those days is fuzzy, but I still remember groping around in the dark of my mind. It seemed that all the color had been sucked out of my life, which was a lie, but that's the way it all looked to me. And felt. Just gray.

I didn't understand why I felt this way. Me, with a happy marriage, nice home, healthy toddler, new baby. Who but a spoiled brat would be crying when she's living any woman's dream? What kind of wife and mother was I anyway?

They call this "rock bottom," I guess. Some people find it at the bottom of a bottle or when they slip their last dollar into a slot machine or when they wake up one morning and realize that they messed up really badly the night before.

But here is where I scraped against my rock bottom: cutting up a red apple for my daughter.

It was 10 P.M., and the baby was finally asleep. My 2-year-old was still awake, though, because I guess I'd forgotten that she had a bedtime. And it shocked me, how I'd forgotten. That self-accusing voice hissed at me, *What kind of mother are you, anyway?* She asked for an apple before she went to bed, so I pulled a Red Delicious from the bottom drawer of the refrigerator.

I remember thinking at the time that I hadn't done anything for her all day long, except cut up this apple. Which was a lie, but I couldn't always tell the difference. I peeled away the skin because she didn't like her apples with skin, and I picked out the seeds.

I handed her the apple slices on a plastic Dora the Explorer plate, and I sat down with her at her tea-party table. Folded into a child's chair, I dropped my head into my hands and sobbed.

Because what kind of mother waits until 10 o'clock at night to do something nice for her child?

I had read about mothers like me—mothers who couldn't cope— in the pamphlets that the nurse gave me before my first baby was born. None of it came true for me, and I was happy with my first baby—always and only happy. But it was different with my second baby, and as I searched for answers, the probable diagnosis pulsed in the soft glow of the internet: postpartum depression.

I read that this condition was "normal." Whatever normal was. But this didn't *feel* normal—waiting until 10 o'clock at night to serve an apple to my child. The online experts said I should seek help.

But, no, I wouldn't ask for help. Not me! What kind of mother of two would be so needy, when mothers of four and five manage just fine?

Later that night, my husband slipped his arm around my waist, pulled me close, and said that it was okay to ask for help. I sobbed into his shoulder. "Why," he asked, "do you always think you've got to do everything in your own power?"

So I called her the next day, my sister in Kansas City. Would she come? Would she drop everything—her life, her own kids—and drive six hours north to help me so I could do more than slice up an apple for my little girl?

The first night she was here, my sister stayed awake all night cradling my crying baby while I slept.

The next day, I went to the doctor, who gave me some pills. When I got home, my sister handed me a piece of white paper. I think now that it was a God prescription. She told me I needed to say the words she had written on the paper every single day, or more often, as needed: "Lord, give me enough grace for today."

She had underlined the word "today."

I went into my bedroom closet that day, and for the first time ever, I fell to my knees before the Lord. I dropped my head onto the carpet in the dark closet beside the laundry hamper. Right there, I aired my dirty laundry to Jesus. My feelings of guilt and despair. My inadequacy. My stiff-necked pride. All of it. I did most of the talking, and he didn't seem to mind.

"Lord, give me enough grace for today," I prayed.

My sister says that on that day, I came out of the bedroom a different woman. She said she didn't know what happened in my room, behind that closed door, but she said I was a new person when I walked out.

I was.

I am.

Yesterday, I was cleaning out the drawers in the kitchen. I found my sister's note in the drawer by the oven, lying under a stack of old catalogs.

I don't take those pills anymore. I would if I needed to, but I stopped years ago. God cleared the gray and brought color back into my life as a mother. For some reason, the day I stopped taking the pills, I tucked my sister's note into this drawer.

I took her note from under the pile, and today, I taped it to the pantry door.

Because who would throw away the handwriting on the wall?

Jennifer Dukes Lee is an award-winning journalist who used to cover crime, politics, and natural disasters. Now, she uses her reporting skills to chase after the redemptive story of Christ. Jennifer is a former news reporter for several Midwestern metropolitan daily newspapers and an adjunct journalism professor at Dordt College in Sioux Center, Iowa. Her husband, Scott, raises crops in northwest Iowa, and together they are raising two girls on the Lee family farm. She is a contributing editor for TheHighCalling. org, and she blogs about faith and family at her blog, Getting Down with Jesus (www.GettingDownWithJesus.com). She is at work on her first book, to be published in 2014 by Tyndale Momentum, an imprint of Tyndale House Publishers.

41

GOD CAN FIX ANYTHING

KAREN ROBBINS

INDEPENDENCE, OHIO

Tennessee's Smoky Mountains lived up to their name as we navigated winding roads up into the mountainside forest, passing through misty clouds while we searched for our turnoff to the cabin we had rented for our vacation.

This would be our first real vacation with our completed family. Everyone was excited. Our twin sons, Rob and Ron, were 12; our third son, Andy, was 9; and we had just adopted Cheryl, age 6, and Don, who was 5 years old.

The kids and all our gear were packed tightly into the station wagon, and I was impressed that there hadn't been too many complaints during the two days it had taken us to drive to Gatlinburg. Some of that composure could have been explained by the fact that Cheryl and Don were still new to our family, and so the "honeymoon" wasn't over yet.

We were still getting to know our two new additions to the family. Cheryl had some learning disabilities but could communicate quite well. Don, on the other hand, had severe developmental disabilities, and his speech consisted more of sounds rather than actual words. But we were beginning to understand him better now that he had been with us for two months. Still, at 5 years old, he could not string together enough words to make a sentence.

Now, as we wound our way through the mountains, large rock out-croppings and tall trees captured the wisps of clouds that hung in the air. But as we climbed higher, the clouds gave way to some sunshine, casting rays of hope for a beautiful day.

Our station wagon was not that old, but it had seen better days. As we ambled up the mountain road, it began to chug and gurgle.

I looked at my husband, Bob. "Please tell me that's just the car shifting gears," I said.

"I can tell you that," he said, "but it won't be entirely true."

On the incline, the car began to slow, and we all held our breath as we neared the top. It slowed to almost a stop. *Would we make it?* Or would we be stuck here in the middle of nowhere with five kids and our vaca-tion hopes dashed? As this point in our lives there were no cell phones, and even if there were, I doubt we could have gotten any service.

With a couple more chugs, we crested the hill and exhaled. So far, so good. The road had leveled a bit and the car seemed to be okay. The noise from the kids in the back seat kicked in again as they talked and played games with each other.

Another incline loomed, and I began silently praying us up it. Again, we made it to the top—just barely, the car slowing along the way until, again, it almost stopped. My nerves were frayed. Bob's knuckles turned white as his hands grasped the wheel.

"I'm going to try to make it to the cabin," Bob said. "It can't be much farther. I'll drop you and the kids off and take the car back down to the first mechanic I can find."

"Okay," I said hesitantly. *Will he be able to make it back down without any trouble?* I wondered anxiously. And how long would I be there in the backwoods with five kids by myself? A dozen scenarios played out in my head, none of them good. This vacation idea of ours wasn't sounding so great any more.

The next mile marker we passed indicated that it wouldn't be too much farther to the cabin, but ahead the road inclined again. Inside, the car grew quiet. The kids felt our tension, and they feared the unknown as much as we did. The station wagon chugged a few times, then gurgled, and then suddenly there was a big bang!

The station wagon lurched forward and began to pick up speed on the hill. We made it to the top with ease, and I heard Bob exhale loudly.

The kids let out a big whoop from the back seat.

A moment later, when they had all quieted down, we heard a small voice.

"G-g-god fixa car!"

It was Don! He had spoken a sentence!

This wonderful sentence came out so clearly that there was no mistaking what he said. Tears brimmed in my eyes. I swiped them away and turned to smile at my new little son in the back seat.

"Yes, Don, God fixed the car." *And God is fixing you too,* I thought. Cars or little boys—God can fix anything.

Karen Robbins is an author and a speaker who lives in Independence, Ohio. She and her husband, Bob, have five children and eight grandchildren. Karen's many interests fuel her desire to write; she is an avid reader, quilter, traveler, and scuba diver. She has published more than two hundred articles and essays and has contributed to many story collections, including Impact *(NPH, 2002),* The Bad Hair Day Book *(J. Countryman, 2006), and* Ho! Ho! Ho! *(J. Countryman, 2006). She has published two novels,* Divide the Child *(Five Corners Press, 1999) and* Murder Among the Orchids *(SmashWords, 2011). Karen's most recent book is her third novel,* In a Pickle *(Martin Sisters, 2012), and she also coauthored* A Scrapbook of Motherhood Firsts *(Leafwood, 2012), which followed* A Scrapbook of Christmas Firsts *(Leafwood, 2008). Karen's blog, Writer's Wanderings, can be found at www.karenrobbins.blogspot.com.*

42

THE DAY OF THE CYCLONES

KRISTEN JOY WILKS

PESHASTIN, WASHINGTON

One of the advantages of being disorderly is that
one is constantly making exciting discoveries.

A. A. MILNE

Our tiny, two-bedroom apartment is the natural habitat of three small boys and one black, 163-pound Newfoundland dog. Within our walls, I have enjoyed story time, snuggling, sweet kisses, and epic wrestling extravaganzas—yet I have also encountered mud, mayhem, and the occasional bout of inexplicable psychosis. When I consider the many perils that my boys have manufactured for my enjoyment over the years, one day immediately springs to mind—The Day of the Cyclones.

At the time, our boys Tigger, Teddy, and Copper were 6, 4, and 2 years old. The day started out fine with our normal homeschooling activities. But I had forgotten that the virtual academy to which we belonged had scheduled a monthly parent-teacher phone conference for that day.

When the phone rang, I told the boys to go play while I turned my attention to Tigger's online teacher. *It's just thirty minutes,* I thought.

What could they possibly do that a quick zip with a vacuum and a couple of paper towels won't cure? I was loathe to use the TV as a babysitter and, after all, I was just five feet away in the other room.

In the middle of the call, I realized that Teddy and Copper had gotten into a kitchen cupboard and opened a package of instant pudding. "NO! Absolutely not!" I hissed before returning blithely—and perhaps blindly—to my phone call.

After I hung up, I discovered that the boys hadn't just opened one packet of pudding. Oh no! They had dumped seven packages of pudding and Jell-O onto the living room carpet and furniture. Then, my three angels poured in half a bottle of hand soap and stirred the mixture into the consistency of artificially sweetened snot.

"Everyone sit on the couch, RIGHT NOW!" I yelled. Yes, yelled. I, who had made it my life's goal to be that one golden, non-yelling parent on the planet.

I tried to vacuum up the mess. My grandparents had given us a truly exceptional vacuum that dumps the dirt into a tub of water, so that dust doesn't billow into the air. But the sticky, soapy soup was impervious to vacuuming and only gummed up the expensive machine. I set the vacuum aside and shut my eyes, trying to regain some measure of calm. I decided to finish our last bit of school, make lunch for my hungry, and now crabby, boys and then plop them in the tub to wash off their full-body coatings of gritty Jell-O granules.

I spent an hour scrubbing the two-foot portion of carpet that had soaked up most of the pudding. Meanwhile, my attention once again diverted, Copper discovered the abandoned vacuum and promptly tipped it over. I cried out in horror as the grubby water pooled out onto my newly scoured carpet.

Through tears of fury I sent up a desperate prayer for help and ordered the boys to stay in their room while I cleaned. But as I scrubbed away, Teddy and Copper had a slight difference of opinion that escalated until Teddy peed into Copper's crib and then bit him, making Copper cry. Not wanting to be outdone, Tigger bit Copper as well, crunching all the way through his diaper and leaving a big bruise on his brother's bottom.

After I freed the three miscreants from their bedroom, the boys gleefully attacked the kitchen, sneaking off with my sugar canister and flinging its contents throughout the kitchen, living room, and stairway. Not content with this spree of destruction, they proceeded to dump out our straw holder, not once, mind you, but twice.

In the living room, I began emptying the bean bag chairs in order to wash the sticky covers. I ran one of the covers downstairs to start a load of wash, and by the time I ran back up the boys had unzipped our large bean bag couch and were scattering fistfuls of upholstery stuffing all over the living room. *Choking hazard!* was my first panicked thought as I rushed about gathering up the little pieces of foam.

The phone rang, and again I marched the boys to their room so that I could answer it. Undeterred, the boys dumped the bathroom trash can into Copper's crib, and when I confined them in the living room so that I could clean the crib, they dumped the office trash across the carpet.

Just then, my husband ran up the stairs all smiles, eager to tell the boys about the "treat" he had just arranged for us. Unbeknownst to me, he had invited friends over for dinner!

Now, I am not a pushover. I dreamed up creative consequences galore, and each time I laid down the law the boys were genuinely contrite. They cried, I cried. Yet still they rampaged.

That day, I was at a complete loss. I have a degree in early childhood education for goodness sake! I had worked in preschools and Bible camps for years, successfully corralling countless children in a calm and loving manner. Yet during that whole horrific affair, I yelled, repeatedly, and at my own sweet boys. On that day of apocalyptic naughtiness, my children discovered that the human face can express at least one hundred shades of furious, and the human voice, one hundred tones of frustration.

But that night, after the boys had all flopped across their beds in destruction-induced exhaustion, I looked at their sweet faces and realized that I had done alright. Not perfectly. I'd made some mistakes. I didn't have the calmest face or voice, but I didn't scream at the top of my lungs either. I don't believe I said anything that will land them in therapy one day. In the end, they snuggled down into their beds with the settled confidence of children who are certain that they are loved. And that was truly an answer to prayer.

All in all, my boys and I survived The Day of the Cyclones. The next morning dawned despite my doubts, and the sun shone down upon a mother and three little boys who were willing and able to try all over again.

Still, I will forever be asking myself, *Why didn't I just pop in a movie!*

Kristen Joy Wilks lives with her camp director husband, three fierce little boys, and an enormous slobbery dog at the beautiful Camas Meadows Bible Camp near Leavenworth, Washington. Kristen is an aspiring writer for teen girls and blogs about the beauty and catastrophe of life at www. kristenjoywilks.com.

43

A Tender Heart

CATHY ELLIOTT

ANDERSON, CALIFORNIA

In memory of my son

I had just stepped into the doorway of my son's bedroom when I caught a ball-like flurry of arms and legs bouncing down the stairs, identifiable by the sparkle of shiny bifocals and a hint of salt and pepper curls flashing past.

My mother. Taking a sudden shortcut.

She rolled to a stop amid scattered plates and unfinished bread crusts, having lost her hold on the trays she was carrying. Mother had just retrieved the lunch dishes from the children's indoor picnic we'd spread out on the upper level of Chris's room. But the four steps down gave her trouble and she tripped, performing several reluctant somersaults. Now she lay on the carpet, wounded, massaging her foot, and attempting a brave face.

My hand flew to my mouth, suppressing a gasp. My poor little mother! That must really hurt. As much as I wanted to be compassionate, though, I could feel that old familiar desire to chuckle tickling my overabundance of funny bones. A lover of slapstick comedy, I saw humor in every pratfall, even when it wasn't meant to be comic relief.

I mean, I really *did* love Lucy. But I couldn't laugh at this, at my sweet mother's mishap. I placed the other hand over my mouth to lock in my amusement.

Don't laugh. Don't laugh. A giggle escaped, and then another.

Soon I was clasping my sides, shrieking with laughter, even emitting an occasional snort, until tears were flowing down my face. My mother looked at me with what appeared to be dazed disbelief and then, probably against her will, the corners of her mouth began to curve upward until she joined in with a giggle or two of her own. Tears were also filling her eyes, but I was sure they were not the joyful kind.

"You and your weird sense of humor," she said, snickering in spite of herself. She continued to rub her foot and groaned a little. "I suppose I did look silly. Still, imagine laughing at someone who just fell down the stairs." She shook her head.

Mother was right. What kind of a daughter was I? But before I had a chance to morph into Florence Nightingale mode, my 10-year-old son, Chris, leapt from the upper level, across all four steps, and landed next to my mother—a superhero without the cape. He knelt down, touching her foot with a gentle hand, and asked, "Grandma, are you okay?"

Mother melted under his tender approach, the empathy causing her tears to flow without restraint.

I, of course, wondered where this boy of mine had gained such a sensitive nature.

If I looked in the mirror, I wouldn't find the role model there. Maybe it was a gift from his grandma; her kindness was legend.

"I'll be all right," she said between little sobs. "I just need to sit awhile."

But she wasn't all right. Mother's ankle quickly swelled beyond her shoe size and began to turn the colors of a vivid sunset, deep yellow and purple. She couldn't walk unassisted, so Dad and I supported her on each side as she limped into the living room and collapsed into a comfy chair. Chris placed a pillow under her foot, now elevated on our ottoman, and patted his grandma's hand.

We served her tea and an ice pack. Chris didn't leave her side, adjusting her pillow support and bringing her magazines. After Mother had downed a dose of aspirin, the family helped her to the car so that Daddy could drive her to their home more than two hours away.

"I'm fine. It just hurts a little now," Mother said, leaning out the back of their big Chevy for farewell kisses. Her foot was propped by the pillow on the bench seat. "I'll keep you posted."

"Grandma, stay off your foot, okay?" Chris lingered at her door. "I'll call you."

Monday came and went with no word from Mother. Chris began to pester me on Tuesday.

"Can we call Grandma today?" he asked.

"She said she'd call. She'll call in her own time." That seemed clear and reasonable to me. In a time before cordless telephones were popular, why make her hobble across a room if she was resting?

By Thursday, I, too, was beginning to wonder what had happened and gave in. When she answered, it was a relief to hear her voice. Soon we were chatting, our voices animated, as we discussed our news. I was just sharing why I didn't like my new perm when Chris appeared, his expression earnest and pleading, indicating that he would like to talk to his grandma. I handed him the phone, cautioning him that Mother and I were not finished visiting. "Don't hang up," I whispered.

He cupped the receiver between tanned hands and plopped on a ladder-back chair in the dining room, one leg swinging back and forth.

"Hi, Grandma," he said. "How is your foot?"

Rats! I had forgotten all about her fall as soon as we started chatting. Mother turned the conversation away from herself, as always, to what interested her children. I felt a rush of shame wash over me as I realized that what had interested me most was mostly—*me*.

Chris gave me a rundown on the doctor's report, placing his hand over the receiver to talk, his voice husky with emotion. Grandma had pulled some ligaments and fractured the bones in the bottom of her foot. Her leg was purple clear to the knee! The doctor was upset because she waited so long to make an appointment. She would be on crutches for weeks.

And I hadn't even bothered to ask.

I looked in wonder at my young son, who was so much more like his gentle grandma. Saying a silent prayer of thanks, I tried to imagine what kind of man he might become. Would he be a great man of compassion, changing the world one heart at a time?

For now, I would settle for a change in myself. A big change initiated by the example of a 10-year-old boy with a tender heart.

Cathy Elliott is the author of two cozy mysteries, most recently Medals in the Attic, *book 2 in the Annie's Attic Mystery Series. She has also published ten educational books for children and written for anthologies and various publications. When she's not spinning tales on her trusty laptop,*

Cathy enjoys antiquing, quilting, and playing her twelve-string guitar. Visit her online at www.cathyelliottbooks.com.

44

DUSTIN DANCED

AMY ROBERTSON

SOUTHERN CALIFORNIA

There are some things learned best in calm, and some in storm.

WILLA CATHER

My youngest son visited me recently. What a wonderful surprise it was—and so completely unexpected!

Dusty has not been away at college. He hasn't been studying abroad, or even bicycling with buddies through Europe. He is not a prodigal son who left our family on bad terms. No, Dustin is simply a child who is afflicted with severe autism.

Like any child, Dusty had his less-than-perfect days, but he was a complete joy to us. He had a smile as broad as a street, and he ran around singing and jumping to music only he could hear. Completely dependent on us and having few language skills, he still was one of the happiest human beings I had ever known. He woke up happy and went to sleep happy. We called him our "little slice of heaven," a light-hearted child who had no earthly worries to weigh him down.

Although Dustin needed care around the clock, he was a joyful and welcome member of our family.

But last year, when he was 10 years old, my happy boy unaccountably disappeared. Dustin became cranky and edgy. He had outbursts of blood-curdling screaming that shocked and frightened us. The doctors couldn't find any medical reason for the change, so we had no choice but to bear it. Shattered, our family tiptoed around on eggshells for months.

One day, Dustin finally exploded into violence at school. He tried to choke two young children on the playground. At home he ran around the house knocking over heavy furniture. He kicked holes in our walls, and choked and bit himself and anyone who came near him.

The doctor prescribed massive doses of Benadryl to calm Dustin, and we had to physically restrain him until he stopped kicking and screaming. I resorted to lying across him for an hour at a time until I was sure he wouldn't hurt himself, his brothers, or me. His outbursts occurred up to five times a day, and they went on unabated for weeks.

My once sweet, happy child had grabbed his bags, slammed the door, and was gone. I didn't even get to say goodbye.

Our family was stunned and weary, and we did the only thing we knew to do. We prayed and we asked everyone we even remotely knew to pray, too. But even in prayer, I wasn't really listening for God. I was overwhelmed with my sorrow and pain, and I was just dumping my laundry list of requests on him. Prayer was a one-way street, and that street was named "Poor Little Amy."

Finally and mercifully, we found a child psychiatrist who specialized in autism. All other treatments exhausted, he prescribed powerful antipsychotic drugs and sedatives to control Dustin's violent behavior.

After about a week, Dustin calmed down and the violence stopped, but the child who was left was not the child I knew. He had a glazed and vacant look, and he was tired most of the time. He drooled uncontrollably for a while. It was better than the screaming, choking, hissing child he had been, though, so we sincerely thanked the Lord.

In time, we had to start Dustin on an even more powerful antipsychotic drug. I expected that he might become even more withdrawn. But one day, I went out to meet Dusty's school bus, and when he stepped off the bus, I could see that it was *him*. The glassy stare was gone, and he looked me straight in the eye. It was crystal clear to me who had climbed down those steps onto the sidewalk—my beautiful, happy son.

Dustin smiled a smile I hadn't seen in more than a year. He was so delighted to see me that instead of walking past me as usual, he came straight over to me and gave me a huge hug. Amazed, I hugged my son tight as tears rolled down my cheeks.

My son's surprise visit had begun.

Dusty and I played all afternoon. I chased him around the house and he squealed with delight when I caught him and covered him with kisses. When my husband returned home from work, we met him at the door.

"Daddy, Daddy!" Dustin exclaimed, as he wiggled and danced around us.

My husband could see that this was not the stony-faced boy of the last eight months.

"He won't stay. It won't last. But isn't it wonderful?" I said through my tears.

"Then let's drink it up while we can," my husband replied.

And so we did.

After the sun set that September night, I found Dustin dancing outside in the dark. He was showered, barefoot, and dressed for bed in a large T-shirt that came down to his knees. With complete abandon, he laughed and sprang on the sidewalk in front of our house. While he spun and skipped, I could see his smile by the blush of the streetlight.

I called to Dustin and opened my arms wide. Without hesitation, Dustin ran and jumped into my embrace. I spun him around a couple of times as he giggled. My heart pounded as I clutched my little one tightly, and I prayed that this moment would last me a lifetime.

At bedtime, I crawled into bed with Dustin. He smiled at me while I traced his features with my finger, and played with his soft brown hair by the light from the hall. Cool tears wet my pillow. "Please Lord, fill me up with these moments," I pleaded. "I need to draw strength from them for the next thousand moments I may never have with him."

And then, it struck me, unmistakable and clear as a bell. *God spoke to me.*

"Amy, can you not see that you are like Dustin much of the time? In your sorrow, you walk right past me. It has been much too long since you ran to me and let me swing you around, clutching you tight. I miss you, and long for you, even more than you long for your son."

I suddenly understood that while Dustin had no choice in whether he connected with me, I could choose to run to my Savior any moment of any day and feel his joy.

Dustin stayed for three beautiful, healing days. In time, he sank deeper into himself, and once again he became glazed and apathetic.

It was so hard to watch him go. My son will not laugh and play with me today, and probably not tomorrow either, and for this my heart aches. But I know now that I have an Abba Father who will hold me tight and swing me around with utter abandon.

Amy Robertson lives in Southern California with her husband, Virgil, and their three sons. She freelances as a scriptwriter and is in the process of getting two books in shape and worthy of publication. A story of hers, "A Closer Look," won the Best Children's Film Award at the 2005 What You See Is What You Get Film Festival. Amy is special projects coordinator for a Christian nonprofit organization, where she plans events and produces in-house products.

NOTE: "Today, at 19 years old, Dustin no longer suffers the outbreaks of violence that plagued him in his younger years," Amy reports. "For that we praise God!"

45

LITTLE BOY LOST

CATHY MESSECAR
MONTGOMERY, TEXAS

I lost my son.

Didn't lay eyes on my 3-year-old for at least seven minutes. It seemed like a lifetime.

If I judged my mothering, I would say that I fit into the mid-range. Not overly cautious or neglectful, perhaps "relaxed" best describes my practice. Let kids be kids. I expected to make mistakes with my first-born. All young mothers do; however, I never thought I'd lose him.

After several rainy days that swelled the creeks and ponds beyond their banks on our 100-plus acres, my son longed to play outdoors. I reveled in his maturity: he was potty trained and farm trained. He knew his mobile boundaries. We had mapped his free-roaming territory, reinforcing it with fencing and frequent warnings: "Russell, don't go out of our yard. Daddy or Mama has to walk you to the barn or the cattle corral."

Cooped up for days in the house, we were beckoned by the musty smell of damp earth into the purity of washed leaves, clean sidewalks, and scrubbed blue skies. However, I also heard the call of dirty laundry: mud-spattered jeans, footprinted throw rugs, and smudged outerwear. I stayed inside and worked my magic with Maytag and Cheer to restore all things cotton, while my son explored the freshly laundered earth within our yard.

Our small home had windows on all four sides, making it easy for me to look outside and locate Russell. I peered out to the backyard and saw him on the swing set. Another peek outdoors and I watched him play with Benji, our Basset Hound. Another look-see found him kneeling and digging in wet dirt with a tarnished silver spoon. Sigh—more clothes to wash.

I folded one load of laundry, and when I looked out my kitchen window, I didn't see Russell. I made a circuit of the windows. I hurried to the back door, threw it open and yelled, "Russell, where are you? Russell, answer Mama!"

Only the sounds of spring chirped back.

I dashed outdoors, ran to the end of our sidewalk, to the gate, Russell's boundary marker. How many times had I pointed at the whitewashed gate and said, "Do not go past here." Do not collect rocks in the driveway. Do not walk to the barn. Do not walk to the garden. Do not. Do not. Do not!

Panic seized me. I hurried into the house and jerked my rubber boots out of the mudroom closet. I pulled them over my damp socks, tugging them on one foot at time as I hopped down the back porch steps. I didn't know where to look. I wanted to look at the right place first. I wanted to see those chubby cheeks. I wanted to see that blond hair. I wanted my son like never before!

Thoughts of pond spillways, the churning creek spanned by a bridge without a railing, the water trough full to the top, a 2,000-pound bull and huge cows grazing nearby fed my anxiety. "Russell!

Russell!" My voice choked on my tears as I called his name. I ran down the driveway toward the creek. Which body of water should I first check?

All the time, I'm calling, "Russell, baby, answer Mama!"

Not a peep. No sign of my only child. That's when I stopped to pray. I actually stopped in my tracks, looked skyward, and said, "Lord, you know where he is. Lead me to him."

When I looked down there was a sign, a roadmap right near my feet. Three tire tracks in the water rivulets and squishy mud led down-hill. I looked back to the open garage where we parked his tricycle. Gone! We had hitched his Radio Flyer wagon to the back of his tri-cycle so he could pull a farm wagon like his grandpa, a dairy farmer. Maybe that's what he rode off to do—his pretend farm chores.

Our land looks like a large flattened out "V." We live at the back of the farm, at the top of one side of the V, with the creek low in the middle. To reach the road, we go up an incline to the V's other high-point near the state highway. Running downhill gave me momentum, and I was at the forested creek before I knew it. The tracks led me to the bridge. I didn't want to look down into the swirling depths, but I had to. I ran to each side of the bridge and gazed down. Relief washed over me when I didn't see flashes of blond boy, chrome handlebars, red grips, or black tires. Finally, past the creek I could see the rest of our farm road leading to the highway.

There. I saw him! Pedaling like a boy on a mission. I rushed uphill for an interception. That's when I also spotted our retired, grand-motherly neighbor, Gloria, standing at the edge of the highway. A large-boned, tenderhearted woman, she had ample room to rest her arms across her bosom—and she looked like a guardian angel, ready to snatch my Russell from harm. Finally, I reached him. He saw my determined face and clamped his sturdy legs around his trike. I lifted Russell off the tricycle seat so fast the bike rattled back to the ground.

As I both hugged and scolded my son, Gloria hollered across the asphalt lanes, "We weren't gonna let him cross the road. We saw him a'comin'. We were watchin' him." I could see her husband, Tony, in the background, ready for backup. Inwardly, I chastised myself for letting too many minutes go between checks on my son. I thanked God for his guidance and for faithful neighbors.

No one ever rears a child alone. A long line of people encircle mothers, protecting, correcting, and teaching our children. A thousand guardian angels that we see and a thousand that we don't see surround our babes. They watch for both dangers and bountiful opportunities. On that day, my son's village grew when watchful eyes aided mine. Dangers had certainly lurked for my runaway on his tricycle—full creeks, lumbering cattle, and speeding traffic. Yet here he was, in my arms.

Thank you, Gloria, for second-nature motherhood, for alert eyes, and for your caring spirit. I lost sight of my son, but due to your help, I had a little boy lost and a little boy found.

Cathy Messecar speaks at local and national women's retreats, women's Bible classes, garden and social clubs, Mothers of Preschoolers (MOPS) groups, and retired teachers and writing guilds. She currently writes for the Courier *and Houston Community Newspapers. She has authored two books with Leafwood Publishers,* A Still and Quiet Soul: Embracing Contentment *(2011) and* The Stained Glass Pickup: Glimpses of God's Uncommon Wisdom *(2006), and co-authored two others with Leafwood,* A Scrapbook of Motherhood Firsts: Stories to Celebrate and Wisdom to Bless Moms *(2012) and* A Scrapbook of Christmas Firsts: Stories to Warm Your Heart and Tips to Simplify Your Holiday *(2008). Learn more about her writing and speaking at www.CathyMessecar.com.*

46

CONFERENCE CALL CUPCAKES

MARGARET EILEEN

BURKE, VIRGINIA

Being a working mom presents its own set of challenges. My life revolves around a meticulous schedule of deadlines, business meetings, social functions, and our children's activities. Yet there are still occasions when an interruption in the schedule can cause my two worlds to collide.

Take September 30th, for instance.

It was my son's eighth birthday and my mommy duty to take cupcakes to school for the 11 A.M. snack time. There, I would spend twenty quality minutes making my son feel special, and then proceed to a 1 P.M. meeting at work, which was approximately forty-five minutes from the school.

Remember those word problems we all did in math class? If a train leaves New York at 7 A.M. traveling at 70 mph, and another leaves Chicago at 10 A.M. . . . . Well, it turns out that these seemingly useless calculations really do have a practical application.

Here's how that day went.

8:40 A.M. The last of my three children leaves for school. Most days I would already be dressed, but I don't want to run the risk of spilling anything on my suit—I'm not exactly Betty Crocker in the kitchen. I grab a quick bite of breakfast and clean up the family breakfast dishes.

8:42 A.M. It's time to start the cupcakes. Most moms would have made them the night before, but I worked late last night and utter exhaustion overtook me. Just as I rip open the Pillsbury cake box, the phone rings. It's a sales rep, one of the forty I support in my region. He has a rush print job and needs my assistance to put it into production.

8:45 A.M. It's a few minutes into the conversation and I can't wait any longer. I prop the phone between my shoulder and chin and set the oven to 325 degrees. The sales rep is still explaining the job specifications while I pour the mix into a bowl, add two eggs, a cup of water, and a quarter cup of oil. Using a noisy electric mixer is out of the question, so I hand stir the batter, listening intently to every painstaking detail of the rep's job.

9:35 A.M. The cupcakes need to bake for thirty-five minutes and cool for another twenty minutes before I can ice them and start off for the school. It's going to be close, but the school is a short two-minute drive up the street.

9:36 A.M. Suddenly, the rep asks a question I can't answer. "Hold on," I say, "I have to conference in the vendor." I put the rep on hold, dial the vendor, find the cupcake wrappers, distribute them into the wells and begin to spoon the batter into the cups. The phone slips off my shoulder and nearly lands in the batter. Fortunately, the call doesn't get dropped along with the phone.

9:52 A.M. We arrive at a course of action for the print job. I hang up the phone and pop the cupcakes into the oven. I throw on my business casual, paint on a face, and even manage to accessorize.

10:19 A.M. The oven timer and the doorbell buzz simultaneously. The dog barks his head off at the friendly alert from the UPS guy that my package has arrived just in time for my 1 P.M. meeting. "Hush up!" I holler to the dog, while I take the cupcakes out of the oven. They look fabulous.

10:20 A.M. I respond to a few emails while I wait for the cupcakes to cool.

10:35 A.M. The cupcakes are still warm, but time is running out. I carefully ice each one and place them into the cupcake carriers. My cupcake carriers were one of those impulse buys that give our husbands ammunition to complain about our spending habits. But buying these carriers turned out to be a stroke of pure genius.

10:46 A.M. Done! I load the cupcakes, my briefcase, and the UPS package into the car and I'm off. A few hundred yards from the house it hits me: No napkins! Showing up at school with a messy snack and no napkins is a major mommy faux pas. I turn the car around and charge back into the house to grab the napkins left over from my daughter's birthday party that I'd put in a baggie. I feel something hard in the bag and discover the number eight candle. I'm grateful for this small victory of forethought. "Matches!" I blurt out loud. Fumbling around in my junk drawers, I finally find them, and I'm off for the second time.

10:59 A.M. I'm almost there. I'm walking—no, running!—across the school parking lot. But if you think I make it with a minute to spare, guess again. Things have changed since we were in school. There are security procedures to follow, forms to sign, and a mandatory self-adhesive visitor's pass to affix.

11:05 A.M. From the main office, I break into a jog to the classroom.

11:06 A.M. Arriving at the door, a cupcake carrier in each hand and a baggie of napkins under my arm, I see my son's face light up. I also see the teacher trying to force a smile as she sneaks a look at the clock. To make matters worse, the Diva of all Room Mothers is volunteering in the classroom today. She and the teacher exchange a pained "She's *finally* here" look.

11:10 A.M. Despite my tardiness, we have time to sing Happy Birthday to my beaming boy and eat our cupcakes. Still, I can't help feeling remorseful. Having twenty-four second graders squirming in their seats for six long minutes must have felt like a punishment—for the teacher, at least, if not for the kids. *Maybe I should have settled for store-bought cupcakes,* I think regretfully. But I had promised my son I would make his favorite flavor—vanilla flecked with colored sprinkles—and you can't buy those off the shelf.

11:25 A.M. We clean up the mess, and by the end of snack time I'm out the door and on my way to my meeting.

I know there are moms who choose to work for the challenge or satisfaction of working, but I'm not one of them. My income is an absolute necessity for our family. My husband is a self-employed contractor who works long hours. The honest truth is that we are only one broken bone away from serious financial difficulty.

Our children have to make some significant allowances because their parents both work. Our 15-year-old son watches our two younger children in the summer when we cannot. I leave a list of chores on the kitchen counter every morning for them to complete. My children know how to empty the dishwasher, pick up after themselves, and run the vacuum.

Most of the working moms I know don't strive to be the best at what they do; they simply try to do the best they can for their families. Keeping up with a job, a home, and children is a juggling act, and sometimes the balls drop. These transgressions, no matter how small, heap a load of guilt on our heads.

I'm proud of myself for putting my children first despite the occasional inconvenience. As a mom, I've learned that it's my smallest accomplishments that give me the greatest joy. So when you get home from work, put down the guilt and pick up your child. Because at the end of the day, it's all about the cupcakes.

Margaret Eileen worked as a print development manager for five years before joining her husband, Brian, as marketing manager of his kitchen and bath renovation company in 2011. She and Brian are the parents of two boys and a girl. She writes short stories and has published a screenplay titled Trusting Faith, *the story of a woman grieving the tragic deaths of her husband and children and what transpires at a house she rents on a solitary vacation. Margaret Eileen is a regular contributor to Faithwriters. com and Christianwriters.com. She blogs at Maggie Moments (www. maggiemoments.blogspot.com), from which "Conference Call Cupcakes" was adapted with permission.*

47

LIGHT OF MY LIFE

TERRI ELDERS

COLVILLE, WASHINGTON

My husband worked rotating shifts for the Long Beach, California, police department the year our son, Steve, started first grade. So, Bob slept mornings and worked evenings. On weekends, he'd often pull a day shift. Our schedules rarely jibed.

"I feel like a single parent," I complained.

"It won't be forever, so try to make the most of it," Bob urged me. "Besides, you'll love having Steve all to yourself."

So for three years, from September to June, life flowed predictably. Steve and I would rise, dress, grab breakfast, and go. Steve trotted off to his school across the street from our apartment complex. I caught a bus to the high school where I taught English.

At dusk, we'd perch together at the kitchen counter of our tiny apartment. Steve plowed through his homework while I corrected papers. Then we'd sizzle up a batch of Jiffy Pop and watch *Ozzie and Harriet* or *The Patty Duke Show*. The steady, plodding backbeat of school bells kept us on track.

In the summer, our days picked up a jazzier syncopated pace. Frequently, we'd ride the bus to the NuPike Arcade at Rainbow Pier, where we'd chuckle with the Laughing Lady who towered over the entrance, or get lost in the maze in the hall of mirrors. After stuffing ourselves with Pronto Pups and salt-water taffy, we'd hit the skee-ball alleys. Often, we'd close our day by treating ourselves to a ride on the double Ferris wheel, where, from the top, we could see all of downtown Long Beach.

Another day, we might visit one of the Ocean Boulevard movie theaters. The first time we exited *Mary Poppins,* we tried to sing "Supercalifragilisticexpialidocious" and got it just as wrong as Jane and Michael did in the film. Steve giggled until he hiccupped. One summer we saw *Born Free*, and Steve ducked his head to hide his tears when Elsa, the lioness, wandered off into Meru National Park.

Sometimes we'd just stroll to our local library to check out stacks of books. Steve had his own library card and favored the Encyclopedia Brown mysteries. On bus trips to the NuPike, the movies, or the park, he'd devise possible ways for the clever boy detective to foil his nemesis, Bugs Meany.

If he were on the day shift, Bob would swing by our apartment on his lunch hour to transport us to a nearby park in his patrol car. We'd pack up sandwiches, and grab a blanket and our books. Steve would play in the sprinklers, climb the monkey bars, and then plop down beside me to discuss Encyclopedia Brown.

After work Bob would rejoin us, bringing along a picnic basket, a Coleman lantern and stove, and our portable radio. We'd broil hot dogs, listen to Vin Scully call the Dodger game, and stay until the mercury vapor lamps flickered on. We'd pack up, and then Steve would turn the dial that slowly snuffed out the wick on the gas-powered lamp.

Bob was right. I enjoyed spending time alone with Steve, witnessing firsthand his developing interests, skills, and attitudes. So, eventually I wanted to have more time for him year round. I quit teaching in 1966 and planned to take a job as a county caseworker in the fall. Though I'd forfeit lazy summers with Steve, my evenings and weekends would no longer be consumed by making lesson plans and correcting homework. It seemed a fair trade.

Steve knew this would be our last full summer together.

"Let's go to the beach more this year. I'm going to save my skee-ball points for something extra special," he said to me.

The summer before, he'd exchanged his points for a Battleship board game. The year before that, a GI Joe action figure and a bag of marbles.

"So what's extra special?" I asked. "A baseball mitt? A chemistry set?"

Steve grinned and shook his head. "I'm not telling . . . you gotta guess."

After three summers, Steve knew how to bowl his nine balls for maximum effect. He'd even bank some balls against the side of the ramp to try to reach the holes with higher point values. His scores steadily improved over the summer—and his tickets piled up.

Shortly before the start of the new school year, Steve and I took our final bus ride to Rainbow Pier.

"I've got a lot of points, Mom. Guess what I'm getting," he challenged me.

"Legos? Roller skates?" I guessed.

Steve shook his head.

"Lincoln Logs? A Daisy Red Ryder Pump Gun?"

Yet another shake of the head and a giggle.

"An electric train?" I asked. "No? I give up. I'm not Encyclopedia Brown!"

Steve chuckled. "You gave up, so you'll just have to wait and see."

To celebrate the summer's end, we splurged on root beer floats at Nathan's. We took a spin on the Looff carousel, even though Steve had protested earlier that at eight he was too old for merry-go-rounds. I insisted that if I wasn't too old for a ride, neither was he.

Finally, we proceeded to the arcade.

"You wait here, Mom."

I watched Steve sprint toward the prize stand, wondering what he'd select. A few minutes later he returned, carrying a bag nearly as big as he was.

"I'll show you what I picked out on our ride home," he said, grinning up at me.

As the bus turned from Ocean Boulevard onto Atlantic Avenue, Steve reached into his bag.

First, he took out a Slinky. I knew a toy like that would barely take a bite out of his accumulated points. Then he dug in again. "And an Etch-a-Sketch."

I nodded, but privately I wondered whether he might have been cheated. I knew he had far more points than those two things cost.

He glanced at me. "And something else," he whispered, ducking his head to one side. He fumbled around inside the bag, and then pulled out a gaudily painted, seashell-encrusted lava lamp.

"I got this for you, Mom," he said. "We've had so much fun at the Pike. The shells will remind you of the beach. And it's turquoise, like the ocean."

"Thank you, sweetheart," I murmured, taking the lamp from him and blinking back a tear. Steve continued to grin.

That fall I started my job as a caseworker, so we never again had entire summers free. My husband eventually returned to working normal day shifts. Steve reached the age where he preferred spending his time playing Stratego and Risk with the boys next door to taking bus trips with his mom.

Decades later, lava lamps became emblematic of 1960s kitsch. Mine, though, remained a cherished treasure—an extra special gift from my extra special son—until it somehow disappeared in our moves from one home to another.

But that incandescent summer of 1966 shines on for me. I'll never forget the warm August sun at the arcade, and those carefree, splashy summer days with my son. He has forever remained the light of my life.

Terri Elders is a licensed clinical social worker who lives near Colville, Washington. Her creative nonfiction has appeared in over fifty anthologies, including Chicken Soup for the Soul, Whispering Angels, Patchwork Path, *and* Thin Threads. *She is a co-creator and editor for Publishing Syndicate's anthology series,* Not Your Mother's Book. *A public member of the Washington State Medical Quality Assurance Commission, Terri received UCLA's 2006 Alumni Award for Community Service for her work with the Peace Corps. She blogs at A Touch of Tarragon (www. atouchoftarragon.blogspot.com).*

48

365 DAYS AND COUNTING

LISA SMITH MOLINARI

MAYPORT, FLORIDA

"You think you got it bad now," other moms cautioned when my kids were young, "just wait 'til they're teenagers."

Like the weird sisters of *Macbeth*, they'd give each other knowing glances and chuckle as they watched me nearly amputate a foot trying get my screaming toddler's stroller onto the escalator at the mall.

I thought those moms were just too old and summarily dismissed their annoying prophecies. Back in the "olden days," I imagined, kids played outside dangerously unsupervised all day while their mothers lounged around in crinoline skirts, smoking cigarettes, polishing silver, and watching *I Love Lucy*.

No wonder their kids turned out to be such horrible teens.

At the time, I firmly believed that whatever stage of parenting I was experiencing was the worst one, and no one was going to convince me otherwise.

This month, my eldest child turned 17, and it occurred to me that only one year of his childhood remains. I'm not sure if I should celebrate or burst into tears.

The first time I held my son in my arms, I felt an awesome sense of love and purpose. In an instant, my own needs shifted from my top priority to a distant second. And the funny thing is, I couldn't have been happier about it. I can't take credit; it was merely a consequence of animal instinct, and like any mama bear, squirrel, or flamingo, the inward focus on my own survival automatically switched to the endurance of my offspring.

Although it is initially a joy to put our children's needs ahead of our own, over time the task of parenting can get bothersome, frustrating, and let's face it, downright terrifying. Nowhere does this fact of life become clearer than in parenting teens. I hate to admit it, but those cackling witches at the mall were right as rain.

When my son turned 13, his head didn't spin, his eyes didn't roll, and foul expletives didn't burst forth from his mouth. No, Hayden was the same kid he'd always been. When he turned 14 we saw subtle changes—his first shave, a deepening voice, a reluctance to accept affection. *How cute,* we thought.

My husband and I drifted contentedly into our son's teen years, comfortably secure that *our* teenager would *never* be a problem, because we were *good* parents and had raised him *right*.

But soon after the candles on our son's Rubik's Cube–shaped fifteenth birthday cake were extinguished, a new period of parenting ensued, which might best be described as "Armageddon."

Suddenly, the bathroom door was permanently locked. Hayden stopped making eye contact. A foul smell hung like a green fog in his bedroom. He snickered secretly into the phone behind his barricaded bedroom door. When we managed to come face to face with him, he was always asleep.

In what seemed like an instant, the sweet boy we had known all these years turned into a smelly, undisciplined stranger who, apparently, hated our guts.

At night we lay in bed, our minds racing with anger, frustration, guilt, and panicked thoughts of our son's future. Desperate, we listened to other parents of teens and found out that the hell we were experiencing was actually quite common.

Apparently, just as new hairs sprout from a teen's body, a budding new attitude develops in the teen brain. The once dependent, reverent child suddenly thinks:

There's nothing that I don't already know. I will now run my own life. I find you totally embarrassing and reserve the right to roll my eyes in pure disgust whenever I see fit. I will, however, continue to associate with you so that you can buy me a car, electronics, clothing of my choice, pizza for me and my friends, and a place to sleep until two in the afternoon. Oh, and don't forget to save upwards of $100,000 to send me off to college so that I can reenact Animal House *at your expense.*

With one year left before my son leaves the nest, you'd think I'd be chilling champagne and making plans to fumigate his room. But ironically, I'm melancholy and must resist the urge to become one of the witches, warning young moms to appreciate the days when their biggest problem is getting a stroller onto the escalator at the mall.

Instead, I'll remind myself that every day of parenting a child is precious, and I'll savor the next 365. And counting.

Lisa Smith Molinari's humor column, "The Meat and Potatoes of Life," appears weekly on her blog, www.themeatandpotatoesoflife.com, and in Stripes Military Moms, *an online supplement to* Stars and Stripes *newspaper. Lisa also writes a self-syndicated Sunday newspaper column and a monthly column for* Military Spouse *magazine. Her work has also appeared in* The Washington Post, *the* Citizen, Houston Women, Arizona Parenting, Northwest Kids, *and the* Village Connector, *among other publications. Lisa formerly worked as an attorney in Pittsburgh, Pennsylvania. She and her husband, active duty naval officer Captain Francis Molinari, are currently stationed at Naval Station Mayport, Florida, with their three children, Hayden, Anna, and Lilly. "365 Days and Counting" first appeared in the* Indiana Gazette *(April 30, 2012) and is reprinted with permission from the author.*

49

Sweet Peas of Mine

DAWN LILLY

NEWCASTLE, WASHINGTON

Whatever my lot,
Thou hast taught me to say,
It is well, it is well with my soul.

HORATIO SPAFFORD

She stood at the edge of the garden, straight-legged and bent at the waist, like a young girl limbering up for a ballet recital. She reached for a flat of seedlings on the ground beside her and I envied her flexibility. She stretched without hesitation, while I flinched at the burn behind my knees. She dug, planted, then patted, all in perfect cadence, as though she moved in rhythm to some song I couldn't hear.

I was mesmerized. Then irritated. She'd planted the sweet peas in the wrong flower bed.

"Mother!" I yelled.

She jumped and nearly lost her balance. Then she turned. All color drained from her face and a fragile old woman stood where once the graceful dancer had.

"Mom . . ." I drew a deep breath, closed my eyes, and slowly counted to ten, mindful of all the times I'd done so with my children.

When I opened my eyes, Mom stood rooted in place, a smudge of dirt streaked across her cheek.

"Why don't you take a break," I said. "Go sit down on the porch."

But she didn't move. She just stared at me with a blank expression on her face. "Did I do something wrong?" she asked.

I surveyed my flower garden and bit back a retort. Plastic seedling pots and Popsicle sticks marking the identity of each sweet pea start littered the ground around her. My detailed chart tracking each seedling's progress over the past three months lay discarded to the side.

I thought I had made myself clear when I told her she could plant the geraniums while I prepared the sweet pea bed. But instead of grabbing the single flat of geraniums, she hauled out every one of my two hundred sweet pea plants. All but a few of my prized seedlings were smashed together in a bed destined for lowly geraniums.

Mom's lip trembled and I blinked back tears of my own. I vacillated, torn between warring emotions. I wanted nothing less than her outright admission of guilt. I wanted her to beg for my forgiveness, to promise to make right what she had destroyed. But as I faced my mother, the woman who had loved me when I was good and loved me no less when I was bad, compassion overcame me.

Ten years ago, I had nearly lost my mom. I arrived at the hospital to find her lovely face swollen beyond recognition. An aneurysm had caused extensive brain hemorrhaging, and I feared that even if she did survive, she'd never be the same again.

While doctors worked frantically to stabilize her for surgery, I withdrew to the corner of the room. I watched. I waited. And I prayed, all the while humming the old hymn, "It Is Well with My Soul." I sang the chorus over and over again, convincing myself that no matter what—life, death, even if only a fragment of my mother remained—all would be well.

Days later, when she lowered her legs to the floor and stood beside her hospital bed for the first time without help, I wept.

"Your mother's a walking, talking miracle," her doctor said from the doorway. "She's tough. A real fighter."

I smiled at Mom and she blushed like a school girl.

I spent the next five weeks at the hospital mothering the woman who had spent her whole life nurturing me. For the first time in our lives, our roles were reversed and the line between mother and daughter blurred.

As the days progressed, it became evident that the brain hemorrhage affected, among other things, my mother's short-term memory, her balance, and her motor skills. The same woman who had recently cartwheeled and rollerbladed with my children now needed help with basic tasks like bathing and combing her hair.

"What was three down again?" Mom asked one afternoon in between yawns.

I set her crossword puzzle aside, reached for the jar of scented lotion on her bedside table, and warmed the fragrant cream between my hands. "How about I rub your legs and feet, Mom? That always relaxes you."

"But I'm not tired." She whined like a 2-year-old as she struggled to keep her eyes open.

I couldn't help but smile. She was no different than my own boys at bedtime. With a few more strokes between her toes, Mom was fast asleep.

And while she slept, I kept watch. I followed the steady rise and fall of her chest. I traced the time-worn creases on her face, skirting the surgeon's expert sutures that criss-crossed half her skull. The face looked the same, but I knew she wasn't the same. She wasn't better. She wasn't worse. She was just different.

"Did I do something wrong?" Mom asked again, drawing me out of my memories and back to the garden. "I just wanted to help."

I looked at the woman I'd loved all my life and had nearly lost long before I was ready to say good-bye. Time. I'd asked God for more time with her, pleaded with him for it, and here I was wasting precious moments fretting over sweet peas.

It made me think: How much time had I lost with my own children? How often had I trivialized fleeting moments fretting over inconsequential things, intent on making a point, or demanding my right to be right, when in the end, it didn't really matter?

I wiped away a tear and smiled.

Mom's face lit up. "I did a good job?"

I nodded. "Perfect. I couldn't have done it any better myself." And to prove it, I buried the last few seedlings beside those she had already planted.

Then I took Mom's hand. "Come," I said, leading her to the garden bench, tucked between lilac bushes covered with fragrant purple blossoms.

Side by side we rested, and I squeezed my mother's hand. "I'm sure glad I didn't lose you," I said. Tears filled my eyes. I blinked and set them free.

Suddenly, Mom straightened with heightened awareness.

"What?" I asked.

"It's just like when you were a little girl."

"What is?"

"This. Us." Mom scanned our lush surroundings. She pointed to the garden where we'd spent the morning weeding and planting. "When you were little, you helped me in my garden. Today, I'm helping you in yours," she said.

Then she took my hand and laid it in her lap. She caressed it like she used to, years ago, when she was Mom, and I, her daughter.

Dawn Lilly has been married to her best friend, Dave, for thirty-five years. She is the mother of two and the grandmother of six. She has written for numerous publications, including Guideposts, Seek, Evangel, *and* Chicken Soup for the Soul. *She has written for DaySpring cards and is currently working on her first novel. Visit her home on the web at www. dawnmlilly.com.*

50

Coming Home . . . Again

PENNY REEDER

MEMPHIS, TENNESSEE

Our only child, our son Chris, was coming home—again. You've probably heard about "boomerang kids." Our Chris was one of them.

After high school, Chris went off to the University of Memphis and tried dorm life, but after a while he came back home. He tried apartment life next, but again returned home. I would like to think home was just so good he could not stay away, but if I'm honest, I'd have to say it was more a matter of economic necessity.

Three years into his college career, Chris decided to take a break from college life and he moved to Nashville, where he worked in a framing shop. Chris is a wonderful artist, so it was a natural fit for his talents. While in Nashville, he attended a church with some friends from college and eventually felt a call to the ministry. His pastor urged him to finish his undergraduate degree and then go on to seminary, so he came back home for the third time.

To be honest, I was worried about how my husband and I were going to adjust to his being home this time. We had gotten used to having our own space and we were both still working, so we had a comfortable routine. We were also caring for our elderly parents, and we had little time for anything else in our lives.

More than that, though, I was worried about Chris. What mother wouldn't be? *Is my baby going to be alright?* He knew he wanted to finish his degree before going to seminary, but then, the question was, how were we going to pay for all of this?

When I'm concerned about something, I'm used to praying about it. And I'm not half-hearted about it either; I pray out loud.

I've experienced the direct presence of the Lord a few times in my life, so I am a firm believer in prayer. We ran a grocery store for almost fifteen years, and whenever money was tight, I'd pray about it. Every time—every single time!—the Lord provided the money we needed to pay our bills or restock the shelves. He'd bring in more shoppers or someone would pay a bill. At the end of the day, the money was always there.

I also used to play the piano for our small country church. One Sunday, I sat down at the piano and was immediately enveloped by darkness. I played and sang the song I'd chosen, and when I got up from the piano, the preacher said, "Well, that was a sermon in and of itself." Yet I knew that it was not me, that the Spirit had come and touched us.

So, when my fears about Chris began building, I knew it was time to take my concern to the Lord. I was driving down the interstate alone one day, and I just began to pray out loud. I prayed at length, talking to God as if he were sitting right there in the car with me.

"Lord, what's going to happen here?" I asked. "How is this going to work out? I need some help here."

As my words died away, a still small voice came to me, as audible to my heart as anything heard in the ear.

I've got this.

Immediately, all my anxiety left me and a beautiful peace flowed through me.

What a gift! Once I finally gave up all control to him, God gave me a blessed peace. I stopped trying to "fix" Chris's life and let God take over. And God did indeed "have this."

One day, in his wanderings, Chris ended up in a pastor's office at a church in Memphis. The church agreed to take Chris into its intern program while he finished his undergraduate studies. They also offered him partial tuition to attend Reformed Theological Seminary in Orlando, Florida. So, he moved to Florida, but he came home now and again for holidays and during summer vacations. After seminary, he worked at a church in Orlando with a pastor who became his close friend and mentor, until he felt called as a chaplain in the Air Force.

My gift of peace has remained to this day, and that's a miracle, too. Chris has been deployed to Afghanistan, and even then my heart was at peace. He moves around a lot for the military, but he loves his work and the Lord has blessed him with a wonderful and godly wife, our daughter-in-law, Jen. They met in Afghanistan, of all places!

We had three and a half wonderful years together with Chris at home. It was a privilege to watch his character develop and to see him bloom and grow in his chosen path. It is a time I will cherish forever.

In my life, I've found that God sometimes does not use a lot of words to get his message across. He does not need to. I don't know what the future holds for Chris and Jen, but I know that God "has this" for my child's whole life, not just for the little time we were blessed to have him at home with us.

Penny Reeder and her husband, Kerry, live in Memphis, Tennessee, and are blessed to be part of the church family at Second Presbyterian Church, the church that helped their son attend seminary. They are both enjoying retirement and looking forward to seeing Chris and Jen whenever possible. Chaplain Reeder recounts how he met his wife in Afghanistan in the story "Tracked Down" in Miracles and Moments of Grace: Inspiring Stories from Military Chaplains *(Leafwood, 2011).*

Acknowledgments

One of the unexpected joys of writing is the opportunity I have with every book to meet dozens of new people. I have many people to thank for helping me find my way to the wonderful storytellers whose work you've just enjoyed.

I want to thank the many authors, speakers, and bloggers who helped me along the way. The wonderful women at Proverbs 31 Ministries spread the word among their ranks. Thank you, Glynnis Whitwer (with whom I also share a publisher and an agent), and thank you, Lynn Cowell. Over at the blog 5 Minutes for Parenting, Annie Schultz put the word out to her writers, leading me to Melanie Ferree Cobb.

My agent Bill Jensen is an ever-flowing fount of entertaining stories—if only you were a mom, Bill! Thanks for letting me borrow some of your talented authors, among them Melanie Shankle, Jennifer Dukes Lee, and Sophie Hudson.

As always, the folks at Leafwood encouraged me throughout the publishing process. This time, they went the extra mile as I searched for stories, introducing me to some of their other authors and even their relatives. It's great to share a publisher with you, Brenda Nixon, Karen Robbins, and Cathy Messecar. Thank you, Phil Dosa, for sending me in the direction of your family.

Thanks are also due to people who have connections with my earlier books and led me to stories for this book: Heidi Bylsma, whose weight-loss story appears in *How We Did It: Weight Loss Choices that Will Work for You*; Lynn Ely, whose father, William D. Cribbs, D.O., contributed a story to *Miracles & Moments of Grace: Inspiring Stories from Doctors*; and Penny Reeder, whose son, Air Force chaplain Chris Reeder, tells a story in *Miracles & Moments of Grace: Inspiring Stories from Military Chaplains*.

In the course of writing the Miracles & Moments of Grace series, I've found two online sources invaluable: Help a Reporter Out and PR Newswire's ProfNet. Thank you, Peter Shankman and Jason Hahn for dreaming up such ingenious ways to connect journalists with great sources.

Lastly, if it weren't for my husband, John, and my son, Evan, I wouldn't be living the life I enjoy as a wife, mother, and writer. To you, I owe my deepest gratitude. And, Evan, keep on eating your veggies and doing your homework so that it'll look like I'm a good mom. You'll find a little something extra in your allowance for your trouble.

Endnotes

1. Pam Guyer lives on Boston's North Shore with her husband, Charlie, and their three children, Kaili, Cameron, and Colby. She is a successful entrepreneur with a home-based direct sales business for Arbonne, a Swiss skin care company. She is passionate about encouraging moms to create a vision for their lives and achieve their goals. She speaks, coaches, blogs at www.livinghipp.com, and has written a book of her empowering concepts, *Living HIPP: Happy, Inspired, Passionate, Peaceful* (Rollem Ink, 2012).

2. *Operating Instructions* (Pantheon, 1993). In this book, Anne Lamott writes about her first year of motherhood with her son, Sam.

3. My two previous books in this series published by Leafwood Publishers are *Miracles & Moments of Grace: Inspiring Stories from Military Chaplains* (2011) and *Miracles & Moments of Grace: Inspiring Stories from Doctors* (2012).

4. *After Life* is a Japanese movie directed by Hirokazu Koreeda that released in 1998.

5. Elizabeth Stone's quote comes from an article in the *Village Voice* by Ellen Cantarow titled "No Kids: My Decision Not to Have Any" (January 15, 1985). In deciding whether to have children, Ms. Cantarow interviewed her friends, including Elizabeth, about their experiences of motherhood. Elizabeth Stone is a professor of English literature at Fordham University and the author of several books, including *Black Sheep and Kissing Cousins* (Transaction Publishers, 2004) and *A Boy I Once Knew* (Algonquin Books, 2002). With Dina Matos McGreevey, she coauthored *Silent Partner: A Memoir of My Marriage* (Hyperion, 2007). Her personal essays and reportage have appeared in *Smithsonian* magazine, the *New York Times*, and the *Chronicle of Higher Education,* among other publications.

6. The story of Mary's encounter in the temple is found in Luke 2:21–40.

Index

Websites and Blogs

Many of the women in this book maintain websites or blogs, where they talk about their lives and their writing or they provide information about their businesses or ministries. All website and blog addresses listed are current as of January 1, 2013.

Betters, Sharon (MARKInc. Ministries)
    www.markinc.org
Butler, Nancy (Above All Else)
    www.aboveallelse.org
Bylsma, Heidi
    www.heidibylsma.com
Cobb, Megan Ferree (Fried Okra)
    www.friedokra4me.blogspot.com
Cornelius, Danielle (Life from a Mom in a Small Town)
    www.adepcornelius.blogspot.com
Cowell, Lynn
    www.LynnCowell.com
Coyne, Sarah (This Heavenly Life)
    www.thisheavenlylife.blogspot.com
Dukes Lee, Jennifer (Getting Down With Jesus)
    www.GettingDownWithJesus.com
Elders, Terri (A Touch of Tarragon)
    www.atouchoftarragon.blogspot.com
Elliot, Cathy
    www.cathyelliottbooks.com
Etole Jones, Susan (Just . . . a Moment)
    www.susan-moment.blogspot.com
Gard, Lori (Pursuit of a Joyful Life)
    www.pursuitofajoyfullife.wordpress.com

Geroy, Annette (Mount Horeb House Ministries)
www.mounthorebministries.com

Gonzalez, Leah (My New Ending)
www.leahs-new-ending.blogspot.com

Grahl, Terry (Enchanted Makeovers)
www.enchantedmakeovers.org

Guyer, Pam (Living HIPP)
www.livinghipp.com
www.pamguyer.myarbonne.com

Hudson, Sophie (BooMama)
www.boomama.net

Kendall, Nikki (Mom on a Mission)
www.nikkiisamomonamission.blogspot.com

Kennedy, Nancy B.
www.nancybkennedy.com

Kimball, Anne (Life on the Funny Farm)
www.annesfunnyfarm.blogspot.com

Kosal, Erica (Bounce to Resilience)
www.bouncetoresilience.com

Lilly, Dawn
www.dawnmlilly.com

Ling, Deb (Christians Be Healed)
http://tinyurl.com/Healing4U

Lyons, Ginger (Buffalo Girls Vintage; Peace, Love & Pearls)
www.facebook.com/pages/Buffalo-Girls-Vintage/134327663376094
www.facebook.com/PeaceLoveAndPearls

Margaret Eileen
www.maggiemoments.blogspot.com

Messecar, Cathy
www.CathyMessecar.com

Nixon, Brenda (The Parent's Plate)
www.toginet.com/shows/theparentsplate

Peña, Andé (Living Out Loud)
www.andepena.com

Robbins, Karen (Writer's Wanderings)
www.karenrobbins.blogspot.com

Schneiter, Rebekah D. (Rebekah-Outnumbered)
www.rebekah-outnumbered.blogspot.com

Scott, Jennifer (Lots of Scotts)
www.lotsofscotts.blogspot.com

Shankle, Melanie (Big Mama)
www.thebigmamablog.com

Smith Molinari, Lisa (The Meat and Potatoes of Life)
www.themeatandpotatoesoflife.com

Staples, Stephanie (Your Life Unlimited)
www.YourLifeUnlimited.ca

Viola, Déa (The Baby Flamingo Co.)
www.thebabyflamingoco.com

Ward, Stephanie (Red Lime Media)
http://redlimemedia.net

Whitwer, Glynnis
www.Glynniswhitwer.com

Wilks, Kristen Joy
www.kristenjoywilks.com

Worth, Hyacynth (Undercover Mother)
www.undercovermother.net

About the Author

First of all, Nancy B. Kennedy is a mom.

Besides her maternal career, Nancy has worked for newspapers and magazines both on staff and as a freelance writer. She worked for Dow Jones in its pioneering computer news service, for which she edited both the *Wall Street Journal* and *Barron's*. Her articles have appeared in the *New York Times*, the online *Wall Street Journal*, and many other national and regional publications. As an editor, she worked for such well-respected publishing houses as Princeton University Press and HarperCollins's Ecco Press.

Nancy is the author of two previous books in the Miracles and Moments of Grace series: *Inspiring Stories from Military Chaplains* and *Inspiring Stories from Doctors*. She has also written a book of weight loss success stories titled *How We Did It: Weight Loss Choices That Will Work for You*. Prior to these books, she wrote two books of children's science activities, and she writes articles and personal essays for books, magazines, and newspapers.

Nancy is a member of the Authors Guild. She and her husband, John, live in Hopewell, New Jersey, with their son, Evan.